VASKO POPA
COLLECTED POEMS

VASKO POPA
COLLECTED POEMS

TRANSLATED BY ANNE PENNINGTON
AND FRANCIS R. JONES

EDITED BY FRANCIS R. JONES

INTRODUCED BY TED HUGHES

ANVIL PRESS POETRY

Published in 1997
by Anvil Press Poetry Limited
69 King George Street London SE10 8PX

This book is published
with financial assistance from
The Arts Council of England

Set in Monotype Dante by Koinonia Limited, Bury
Printed at Alden Press Limited
Oxford and Northampton
Distributed by Password, Manchester

ISBN 0 85646 237 3 hbk
ISBN 0 85646 268 3 pbk

A catalogue record for this book
is available from the British Library

This translation has been made possible
in part through a grant from
the Wheatland Foundation, New York

for Haša

CONTENTS

BARK (*1953*)

SECONDARY HEAVEN (1968)

EARTH ERECT (1972)

THE HOUSE IN THE HIGHROAD (1975)

from IRON GARDEN *(unpublished)*

The Little Box

EDITOR'S PREFACE

Vasko Popa's friend and translator, Anne Pennington, died on my wedding day in 1981. At the time she was working on a draft version of Popa's *The Cut*: this task I took over the following year, a published version appearing in 1986 in *Poetry World 1*. In 1987 Vasko Popa and Peter Jay, Anne Pennington's literary executor and chief editor of the Anvil Press, asked me to prepare an expanded and updated version of the 1978 *Collected Poems*.

My aim has been to include all the poems from Vasko Popa's 1988 collected works, *Dela*. The 1978 edition had omitted a number of poems from *Bark*, all of them in the *Far Within Us* cycle, and several poems from *The House in the Highroad*. These have now been translated; *The Cut* and the poems making up the *Little Box* cycle have also been added. I have also written a comprehensive set of notes to the poems, both to explain insoluble translation problems and to help the reader to understand the complex symbolic universe of Popa's 'middle period'.

The bulk of the translations remains by Anne Pennington. Where appropriate, I have edited these in accordance with her own marginal comments in her copy of *Collected Poems*, keeping changes of my own to the minimum. A few poems, however – indicated in the index – are based on a more extensive reworking of Anne Pennington's originals: *The Cut*, where many of my final versions derive from Anne Pennington's drafts, accounts for the majority of these.

In addition, I have transcribed all Serbo-Croat proper nouns back into standard *latinica* orthography (e.g. 'Vršac' instead of 'Vershats' unless an accepted English version exists (hence 'Belgrade', not 'Beograd'). A pronunciation guide is at the back of the book.

FRANCIS R. JONES

INTRODUCTION

Vasko Popa is one of a generation of East European poets – Holub of Czechoslovakia and Herbert of Poland are perhaps two others of similar calibre – who were caught in mid-adolescence by the war. Their reaction to the mainly surrealist principles that prevailed in Continental poetry in the inter-war years was a matter of personal temperament, but it has been reinforced by everything that has since happened, to their countries in particular and in some measure (more than ever before) to human beings everywhere. Circumstantial proof that man is a political animal, a state numeral, as if it needed to be proved, has been weighed out in dead bodies by the million. The attempt these poets have made to record man's awareness of what is being done to him, by his own institutions and by history, and to record along with the suffering their inner creative transcendence of it, has brought their poetry down to such precisions, discriminations and humilities that it is a new thing. It seems closer to the common reality, in which we have to live if we are to survive, than to those other realities in which we can holiday, or into which we decay when our bodily survival is comfortably taken care of, and which art, particularly contemporary art, is forever trying to impose on us as some sort of superior dimension. I think it was Miłosz, the Polish poet, who when he lay in a doorway and watched the bullets lifting the cobbles out of the street beside him realized that most poetry is not equipped for life in a world where people actually do die. But some is. And the poets of whom Popa is one seem to have put their poetry to a similar test.

We can guess at the forces which shaped their outlook and style. They have had to live out, in actuality, a vision which for artists elsewhere is a prevailing shape of things but only brokenly glimpsed, through the clutter of our civilized liberal confusion. They must be reckoned among the purest and most wide awake of twentieth century poets.

In a way, their world reminds one of Beckett's world. Only theirs seems perhaps braver, more human and so more real. Beckett's standpoint is more detached, more analytical, and more the vision of an observer, or of the surgeon, arrived at through private perseverance. Their standpoint, in contrast, seems that of participants. It shows the positive, creative response to a national experience of disaster, actual and prolonged, with an endless succession of bitter events. One feels behind each of these poets the consciousness of a people. At bottom, their vision, like Beckett's, is of the struggle of animal cells and of the torments of spirit in a world reduced to that vision, but theirs contains far more elements than his. It contains all the substance and feeling of ordinary life. And one can argue that it is a step or two beyond his in imaginative truth, in that whatever terrible things happen in their work happen within a containing passion – Job-like – for the elemental final beauty of the created world. Their poetic themes revolve around the living suffering spirit, capable of happiness, much deluded, too frail, with doubtful and provisional senses, so undefinable as to be almost silly, but palpably existing, and wanting to go on existing – and this is not, as in Beckett's world, absurd. It is the only precious thing, and designed in accord with the whole universe. Designed, indeed, by the whole universe. They are not the spoiled brats of civilization disappointed of impossible and unreal expectations and deprived of the revelations of necessity. In this they are prophets speaking somewhat against their times, though in an undertone, and not looking for listeners. They have managed to grow up to a view of the unaccommodated universe, but it has not made them cynical, they still like it and keep all their sympathies intact. They have got back to the simple animal courage of accepting the odds.

In another way, their world reminds one of the world of modern physics. Only theirs is more useful to us, in that while it is the same gulf of unknowable laws and unknowable particles, the centre of gravity is not within some postulate deep in space, or leaking away down the drill-shaft of mathematics, but inside man's sense of himself, inside his body and his essential human subjectivity. They refuse to sell out their arms, legs, hair, ears, body and soul and all it has suffered with them, in order to escape with some fragmentary sense, some abstract badge of self-estrangement, into a popular membership safety. In their very poetic technique – the infinitely flexible, tentative, pragmatic freedom with which they handle their explorations – we read a code of wide-openness to what is happening, within or without, a careful refusal to seal themselves off from what hurts and carries the essential information, a careful refusal to surrender themselves to any mechanical progression imposed on them by the tyranny of their own words or images, an endless scrupulous alertness on the frontiers of false and true. In effect, it is an intensely bracing moral vigilance. They accept in a sense what the prisoner must accept, who cannot pretend that any finger is at large. Like men come back from the dead they have an improved perception, an unerring sense of what really counts in being alive.

This helplessness in the circumstances has purged them of rhetoric. They cannot falsify their experience by any hopeful effort to change it. Their poetry is a strategy of making audible meanings without disturbing the silence, an art of homing in tentatively on vital scarcely perceptible signals, making no mistakes, but with no hope of finality, continuing to explore. Finally, with delicate manoeuvring, they precipitate out of a world of malicious negatives a happy positive. And they have created a small ironic space, a work of lyrical art, in which their humanity can respect itself.

Vasko Popa uses his own distinctive means. Like the others, he gives the impression of being well-acquainted with all that civilization has amassed in the way of hypotheses. Again, like the others, he seems to have played the film of history over to himself many times. Yet he has been thoroughly stripped of any spiritual or mental proprietorship. No poetry could carry less luggage than his, or be freer of predisposition and preconception. No poetry is more difficult to outflank, yet it is in no sense defensive. His poems are trying to find out what does exist, and what the conditions really are. The movement of his verse is part of his method of investigating something fearfully apprehended, fearfully discovered. But he will not be frightened into awe. He never loses his deeply ingrained humour and irony: that is his way of hanging on to his human wholeness. And he never loses his intense absorption in what he is talking about, either. His words test their way forward, sensitive to their own errors, dramatically and intimately alive, like the antennae of some rock-shore creature feeling out the presence of the sea and the huge powers in it. This analogy is not so random. There is a primitive precreation atmosphere about his work, as if he were present where all the dynamisms and formulae were ready and charged, but nothing created – or only a few fragments. Human beings, as visibly and wholly such, rarely appear in Popa's landscapes. Only heads, tongues, spirits, hands, flames, magically vitalized wandering objects, such as apples and moons, present themselves, animated with strange but strangely familiar destinies. His poetry is near the world of music, where a repository of selected signs and forms, admitted from the outer world, act out fundamental combinations that often have something eerily mathematical about their progressions and symmetries, but which seem to belong deeply to the world of spirit or of the heart. Again like music, his poems turn the most grisly confrontations into something deadpan playful: a spell, a riddle, a game, a story. It is the Universal Language behind language, and when the poetic texture of the verbal code has been cancelled (as it must be in translation, though throughout this volume the translations seem to me extraordinary in poetic rightness and freshness) we are left with solid hieroglyphic objects and events, meaningful in a direct way, simultaneously earthen and spiritual, plain-statement and visionary.

He arrived at this freedom and inevitability gradually. His earliest manner often owes a lot to a familiar kind of mildly surrealist modern poesy, though it is charming in Popa, and already purposeful, as in the poem entitled 'In Forgetting', which is from a series of landscapes:

> From the distant darkness
> The plain stuck out its tongue
> That irrepressible plain
>
> Spilt events
> Strewn faded words
> Levelled faces

Here and there
A hand of smoke

Sighs without oars
Thoughts without wings
Homeless glances

Here and there
A flower of mist

Unsaddled shadows
More and more quietly paw
The hot ash of laughter

That is from his first book, *Kora*, but 'Acquaintance', the first poem in
the same book, already sketches out the essential method and uni-
verse of his later and more characteristic work:

Don't try to seduce me blue vault
I'm not playing
You are the vault of the thirsty palate
Over my head

Ribbon of space
Don't wind round my legs
Don't try to entrance me
You are a wakeful tongue
A seven-forked tongue
Beneath my steps
 I'm not coming

My ingenuous breathing
My breathless breathing
Don't try to intoxicate me
I sense the breath of the beast
I'm not playing

I hear the familiar clash of dogs
The clash of teeth on teeth
I feel the dark of the jaws
That opens my eyes
I see

I see
I'm not dreaming

It is all there, the surprising fusion of unlikely elements. The sophisticated philosopher is also a primitive, gnomic spell-maker. The desolate view of the universe opens through eyes of childlike simplicity and moody oddness. The wide perspective of general elemental and biological law is spelled out with folklore hieroglyphs and magical monsters. The whole style is a marvellously effective artistic invention. It enables Popa to be as abstract as man can be, yet remain as intelligible and entertaining and as fully human as if he were telling a comic story. It is in this favourite device of his, the little fable of visionary anecdote, that we see most clearly his shift from literary surrealism to the far older and deeper thing, the surrealism of folklore. The distinction between the two seems to lie in the fact that literary surrealism is always connected with an extreme remove from the business of living under practical difficulties and successfully managing them. The mind, having abandoned the struggle with circumstances and consequently lost the unifying focus that comes of that, has lost morale and surrendered to the arbitrary imagery of the dream flow. Folk-tale surrealism, on the other hand, is always urgently connected with the business of trying to manage practical difficulties so great that they have forced the sufferer temporarily out of the dimension of coherent reality into that depth of imagination where understanding has its roots and stores its X-rays. There is no sense of surrender to the dream flow for its own sake or of relaxation from the outer battle. In the world of metamorphoses and flights the problems are dismantled and solved, and the solution is always a practical one. This type of surrealism, if it can be called surrealism at all, goes naturally with a down-to-earth, alert tone of free inquiry, and in Popa's poetry the two appear everywhere together.

The air of trial and error exploration, of an improvised language, the attempt to get near something for which he is almost having to invent the words in a total disregard for poetry or the normal conventions of discourse, goes with his habit of working in cycles of poems. He will trust no phrase with his meaning for more than six or seven words at a time before he corrects his tack with another phrase from a different direction. In the same way, he will trust no poem with his meaning for more than fifteen or so lines, before he tries again from a totally different direction with another poem. Each cycle creates the terms of a universe, which he then explores, more or less methodically, with the terms. And one of the attractions of all Popa's poems is that one cannot set any limit to how deeply into the substance of the universe his intuitions may penetrate. They are often reminiscent of Kekulé's whirling dream snake. The cycle called 'Games', for instance, is close to mankind as we know it. Nothing prevents these poems from being merely ingenious, or virtuoso pieces of phrasing and timing, except the shock of recognition they impart, and the universe of grim evil which they evoke. It could as well be protozoa, or mathematical possibilities, playing these games, as anything in humanity. They are deeper than our reality as puppets are deeper than our reality: the more human they look and act the more elemental they seem.

In *Secondary Heaven* (1968), the total vision has become vast and one understands why he has been called an epic poet. His cosmos is more mysteriously active and dreadful but his affection for our life is closer than ever. The infinite terrible circumstances that seem to destroy man's importance, appear as the very terms of his importance. Man is the face, arms, legs, etc., grown over the infinite, terrible All. Popa's poems work in the sanity and fundamental simplicity of this fact, as it might appear to a man sitting in a chair.

Earth Erect, published in 1972, is a poetic commentary on the historical folk-memory of the Serbs, a poem of pilgrimage through sacred national places and events, and revolving around St Sava, the patron saint of Serbia and mythical shepherd of the wolves. Applied to such material, Popa's methods produce a marvellously rich busily-working pattern of associations, with large, sudden openings through history and weird resonances of tribal feeling. At the same time the whole sequence operates, with even greater intensity, as an organic sequence of dream-visions, drawing on many sources, charged with personal feeling, an alchemical adventure of the soul through important changes. It is a unique display of his art, to produce a national poem, a psychological adventure, a tribal dream of mythical density, and a private commentary on history, all in the same brief words, and simultaneously create a chain of such intensely beautiful artefacts.

In 1975 he published three long cycles. *Wolf Salt* drew on the same lode of material as *Earth Erect*, but in a slightly different way. This is surely one of the most fascinating collections. The lame wolf is the modern Serb, and the Lame World is the spirit of the Serbs. The poems are lame-wolf psalms addressed – in many moods and with much shape-shifting – to the mythical Lame Father or Mother of all Serb-Wolves. It is the real thing, a call to a whole people, in the profoundest kind of language. And a call to the Ancestral Spirit of a whole people. The way to read it, perhaps, is as something in the same category of literary production as David's *Psalms*. But the motive, and the serious weight of the work, is by the way. Whatever else it may be, it is for us a book of Popa's poems at their best – entertaining, infinitely inventive, and beautiful.

A few wolf-poems spill over into *Raw Flesh*, another group of poems published in 1975 and written during the same period as *Wolf Salt*. These are unlike anything Popa had published before: simple direct jottings evoking memories of the war years and the town of Vršac. Except for the poems relating to his earliest childhood and forebears, where the wolves appear, these poems are without mythical dimension. But unfailingly they stretch wings towards the wider legendary worlds of the other books, setting themselves into the bigger settings.

All Popa's collections echo among each other. One feels the large consistent wholeness behind the swarming parts. The third collection published in 1975, *The House in the Highroad*, was written over the preceding twenty years. None of his tightly consistent cycles seems to have been written at one go, on a single inspiration. They have smouldered along through years, criss-crossing each other, keeping the character of their own genes, working out their completeness. Popa's imaginative journey resembles a Universe passing through a Universe. It has been one of the most exciting things in modern poetry, to watch this journey being made.

TED HUGHES
1977

TRANSLATOR'S PREFACE

Vasko Popa sometimes writes as if he were working at a huge jigsaw puzzle, already in existence, but which only he can put together in a visible – or audible – form. Each word, each poem is a discovery which must be put in its right place in relation to all the other pieces and Popa seems to have an astonishing grasp of what the complete picture will look like. The translator here has a special problem: in the search for the best shade of meaning one must take account of the context of each word, but with Popa the context is, to some extent, the whole of his work, both written and unwritten. The collaboration of the poet is, of course, immensely valuable, since Popa, without revealing his vision of future discoveries, is able to bring his translator back from fanciful leaps in the wrong direction.

Some of the depth and power of Popa's poetry comes from his treatment as real objects and real beings of what appear at first to be mere symbols or metaphors: the quartz pebble is a real stone, hard, round, splittable; the lame wolf is not an abstract god-idea, he is a wounded four-footed beast, who may be expected to growl and lash his tail and bite. This means that the translator cannot be satisfied with a near-equivalent in the English version, nor try to elucidate the message by using a parallel from a more familiar culture — however strange St Sava may be for an English reader, he cannot be replaced by St George.

Popa's language is extremely rich and imaginative; except for special effect he avoids terms recently borrowed and smacking of the international urban culture; he prefers older, native Slavonic words for which he draws on mediaeval literature, folk poetry, charms, riddles, games and legends; sometimes he also invents new compounds on traditional models. He manages to do this without becoming obscure or artificially folksy; he is not trying to take the language back into an older period, but is enriching it and showing a way forward. Much of this folk flavour is lost in the English translation, since English literary usage is too far removed from our folk tradition to mingle with it happily; literary Serbo-Croat was formed as recently as the early nineteenth century and was firmly based on the spoken language and popular literature. Popa is true to this popular tradition without strained archaizing in a way which in English seems impossible.

Popa is notably economical in his use of language: words are chosen and placed with masterly precision, so that the message is conveyed clearly without the help (or distraction) of punctuation. English, with its articles and lack of inflections, almost always needs to use more words than Serbo-Croat, and the general effect of the English translation is also influenced by the larger number of short words and of words ending in consonants — Serbo-Croat has few single-syllable words and the majority of its forms end in vowels. In this poetry it is essential to bring out the exact meaning of words and so there has been no attempt to imitate the sound patterns of the original, although, of course, the aim has been to find a tone which Popa might have used had he written in English.

Obedience is surely a translator's cardinal virtue, but obedience to a poet does not mean the slavish translation of individual words; on the contrary, it requires the grasp of the most important features of the poet's work so that, whatever else is lost, these may be faithfully transmitted in the translating language. Vasko Popa's great mastery of his language and of his matter, the many-sidedness and complexity of his messages make the task of translating him difficult but enormously interesting and rewarding. The translator hopes that these versions convey enough of the force of the originals for the English reader to appreciate and enjoy the work of this very remarkable poet.

The translator would like to acknowledge the help of Vasko Popa and the advice and encouragement of Peter Levi and Daniel Weissbort.

ANNE PENNINGTON
1977

ANNE PENNINGTON

Until her last breath she enlarges
Her Oxford house
Built in Slavonic
Vowels and consonants

She polishes the corner-stones
Until their Anglo-Saxon shine
Begins to sing

Her death is like a short breath-stop
Under the distant limetrees of her friends

Cambridge, 5 June 1981

translated by Peter Jay,
Anthony Rudolf and Daniel Weissbort

BARK

ACQUAINTANCE

Don't try to seduce me blue vault
I'm not playing
You are the vault of the thirsty palate
Over my head

Ribbon of space
Don't wind round my legs
Don't try to entrance me
You are a wakeful tongue
A seven-forked tongue
Beneath my steps
I'm not coming

My ingenuous breathing
My breathless breathing
Don't try to intoxicate me
I sense the breath of the beast
I'm not playing

I hear the familiar clash of dogs
The clash of teeth on teeth
I feel the dark of the jaws
That opens my eyes
I see

I see
I'm not dreaming

CONVERSATION

Why do you rear up
And desert the tender shores
Why O my blood

Where should I send you
To the sun

You think the sun kisses
You've no idea
My buried river

You're hurting me
Carrying away my sticks and stones
What ails you my whirligig

You'll spoil my infinite circle
That we haven't finished building yet
My red dragon

Only flow further
So the feet don't walk off with you
Flow as far as you can O my blood

THE IRON APPLE TREE

Where is my peace
Impenetrable peace

The iron apple tree
Has pierced my skull with its trunk
I gnaw at it
I have gnawed away my jaws

With its leaves it fettered me
I browse on them
I have browsed away my lips

With its branches it hobbled me
I try to break them
I have broken my fingers

Where is my peace
Unbreakable peace

The iron apple tree
Has sent down its roots
Deep into my soft rock
I pull at them
I have pulled out my entrails

With its cruel fruit it fattens me up
I bore into them
I have bored through my brain

Where is my peace
To be the iron apple tree's
First rust and last autumn

Where is where is my peace

ECHO

The empty room begins to growl
I withdraw into my skin

The ceiling begins to yelp
I fling it a bone
The corners begin to yap
To each I fling a bone
The floor begins to bay
I fling it a bone too

One wall begins to bark
To it I fling a bone
And the second and third and fourth walls
Begin to bark
I fling each one a bone

The empty room begins to howl
And I myself empty
Without a single bone

Turn into a hundredfold
Echo of the howling

And echo echo
Echo

DEPARTURE

I'm no longer here
I haven't moved from the spot
But I'm not here now

Let them come in
Let them look let them search

The watermill in the shadow of the ribs
Grinds the ripe void
Fag ends of cheap dreams
Smoulder in the ashtray
I'm no longer here

A moored boat rocks
On the red waves
A few unripened words
Hang in the cloudy throat
I'm no longer here

I haven't moved from the spot
But I'm far away now
They'll scarcely catch me

JOURNEY

I journey
And the highway journeys too

The highway sighs
A deep dark sigh

I have no time for sighing
I journey further

No longer stumbling
Over sleeping stones on the highway
I journey lighter

No longer does the work-free wind
Delay me with chatter
It's as if he couldn't see me
I journey faster

My thoughts tell me I have left
Some bloody some dull pain
At the bottom of the abyss behind me

I have no time for thinking
I journey

[1943–1945]

IN THE ASHTRAY

A tiny sun
With yellow tobacco hair
Is burning out in the ashtray

The blood of cheap lipstick suckles
The dead stumps of stubs

Beheaded sticks yearn
For sulphur crowns

Blue roans of ash whinny
Arrested in their prancing

A huge hand
With a burning eye in its palm
Lurks on the horizon

IN A SIGH

On roads from the depths of the soul
On blue-black roads
Weed travels
The roads disappear
Beneath its steps

The pregnant crops
Are raped by swarms of nails
The furrows have vanished
From the field

Invisible lips
Have wiped out the field

Space is overjoyed
Staring
At its smooth hands
Smooth and grey

ON THE TABLE

The tablecloth stretches
Into infinity

The ghostly
Shadow of a toothpick follows
The bloody trail of the glasses

The sun clothes the bones
In new golden flesh

Freckled
Satiety scales
The breakneck crumbs

Buds of drowsiness
Have burst through the white bark

IN A GROAN

The flame spurted high
From the abyss in the flesh

Beneath the earth
An impotent fluttering of wings
And a blind scrabbling of paws

On the earth nothing

Beneath the clouds
The weak lamps of gills
And the wordless screams of algae

ON THE HATSTAND

The collars have bitten through
The necks of hanged emptiness

Second thoughts hatch out
In the warm hats

Fingers of twilight peep
From the widowed sleeves

Green terror sprouts
In the tame pleats

IN FORGETTING

From the distant darkness
The plain stuck out its tongue
That irrepressible plain

Spilt events
Strewn faded words
Levelled faces

Here and there
A hand of smoke

Sighs without oars
Thoughts without wings
Homeless glances

Here and there
A flower of mist

Unsaddled shadows
More and more quietly paw
The hot ash of laughter

ON THE WALL

Long ago
The first whiteness melted away

The wrinkles of time
Pullulated
On the bountiful wilderness

An unkissed field

Idle forms
Disguised
In the fleece of surprise

An unplayed game

A hundred-headed superfluity
On the eternal pasture

ON THE HAND

On the quicksand
Dumb crossroads
Hesitating

At each crossroad
An inquisitive glance
Changed to a standing-stone

Rosy desert

But all that comes to it
Bursts into bud with sense
Bursts into flower with hope

A unique spring
Or a blessed mirage

IN A SMILE

At the corners of the lips
Has appeared a golden ray

Waves are dreaming
In bushes of flames

Blue-eyed distances
Have coiled up into a ball

Noon is ripening peacefully
In the very heart of midnight

Tame thunderbolts are buzzing
Above the leaves of quietness

DUCK

She waddles through the dust
In which no fish are smiling
Within her sides she carries
The restlessness of water

Clumsy
She waddles slowly
The thinking reed
Will catch her anyway

Never
Never will she be able
To walk
As she was able
To plough the mirrors

HORSE

Usually
He has eight legs

Between his jaws
Man came to live
From his four corners of earth
Then he bit his lips to blood
He wanted
To chew through that maize stalk
It was all long ago

In his lovely eyes
Sorrow has closed
Into a circle
For the road has no ending
And he must drag behind him
The whole world

DONKEY

Sometimes he brays
Rolls in the dust
Sometimes
Then you notice him

Otherwise
You see only his ears
On the head of the planet
But he's not there

PIG

Only when she felt
The savage knife in her throat
Did the red veil
Explain the game
And she was sorry
She had torn herself
From the mud's embrace
And had hurried so joyfully
From the field that evening
Hurried to the yellow gate

HEN

She believes
Only the merry cheeping
Of her yellow memories

She vanishes
Before the snowy branches
That reach out for her

She dries up
Beneath the hungry lakes
That circle above her

She jumps away
From her bloody head
Which thrusts her into night

She jumps away
To fly up to her roost

DANDELION

On the edge of the pavement
At the end of the world
The yellow eye of loneliness

Blind steps
Beat down his neck
Into the stone belly

Underground elbows
Drive his roots
Into the black earth of the sky

A dog's lifted leg
Mocks him
With an overheated shower

His joy is only
A stroller's homeless glance
Which spends the night
In his corolla

And so
The stub burns out
On the lower lip of impotence
At the end of the world

CHESTNUT TREE

The street boozes away
All his green bank-notes
Whistles bells and horns
Weave nests in his crown
Spring prunes his fingers

He lives on the adventures
Of his unreachable roots
And on the wonderful memories
Of the surprise nights
When he vanishes from the street

Who knows where he goes

He'd get lost in a wood
But always by dawn
He's back in his place in the row

CREEPER

The daintiest daughter
Of the green underground sun
She would escape
From the wall's white beard
Rise upright in the marketplace
In all her beauty
With her serpentine dance
Seduce the storm-winds
But the broad-shouldered air
Doesn't offer his arm

MOSS

Yellow sleep of absence
From the naive tiles
Waits

Waits to descend
On earth's closed eyelids
On houses' extinguished faces
On trees' meek arms

Waits unnoticed
To draw
Over the widowed furniture beneath him
Carefully
A yellow dust-sheet

CACTUS

He pricks
The rosy cloud of the hand
Even the rain lies

He pricks the red-hot tongues
Of mules and the sun
Even the sky kisses with knives

He will not marry off his shadow
Even the wind deceives with the beauty of distances

He pricks the complacent thighs
Of knowing nights and innocent waves
He will not find a wife for his green laughter
Even the air bites

The crag that gave him birth
Is right
He pricks pricks pricks

POTATO

Mysterious murky
Face of earth

He speaks
With midnight fingers
The language of eternal noon

He sprouts
With unexpected dawns
In his larder of memories

All because
In his heart
The sun sleeps

CHAIR

The weariness of wandering hills
Gave its shape
To her sleepy body

She's always on her feet

How she would love
To dash downstairs
Or dance
In the moonlight of the skull
Or just sit down
Sit down on someone else's curves of weariness
To rest

PLATE

A yawn of free lips
Above the horizon of hunger
Below the blind mark of satiety

A sleepwalker's yawn
Amid the toothy flow
And the sleepy ebb

A haughty porcelain yawn

In a golden ring of boredom
Patiently awaits
The inevitable tornado

PAPER

for Aurèle Gavrilov

Along the fruitful pavements
Nausea gathers
The surviving smiles
Of raped objects

On the wind's gentle slopes
It grasps at
Clean flights
Without departure or return

Beneath the seasons' eyebrows
It picks
The only leaf
Faithful to the absent branches

In vain

QUARTZ PEBBLE

for Dušan Radić

Headless limbless
It appears
With the excitable pulse of chance
It moves
With the shameless march of time
It holds all
In its passionate
Internal embrace

A smooth white innocent torso
It smiles with the eyebrow of the moon

[1951]

1

We raise our arms
The street climbs into the sky
We lower our eyes
The roofs go down into the earth

From every pain
We do not mention
Grows a chestnut tree
That stays mysterious behind us

From every hope
We cherish
Sprouts a star
That moves unreachable before us

Can you hear a bullet
Flying about our heads
Can you hear a bullet
Waiting to ambush our kiss

2

Look here's that uninvited
Alien presence look it's here

A shudder on the ocean of tea in the cup
Rust taking hold
On the edges of our laughter
A snake coiled in the depths of the mirror

Will I be able to hide you
From your face in mine

Look it's the third shadow
On our imagined walk
Unexpected abyss
Between our words
Hoofs clattering
Below the vaults of our palates

Will I be able
On this unrest-field
To raise you a tent of my hands

3

Unquiet you walk
Along the rims of my eyes

On the invisible grating
Before your lips
My naked words shiver

We steal moments
From the unheeding iron saws

Your hands sadly
Flow into mine
The air is impassable

4

Green gloves rustle
On the avenue's branches

The evening carries us under its arm
By a path which leaves no trace

The rain falls on its knees
Before the fugitive windows

The yards come out of their gates
And stand looking after us

5

The nights are running out of darkness

Steel branches grasp
The arms of passers-by

Only anonymous chimneys
Are free to walk the streets
Which slice across our sleeplessness

In the gutters our stars decay

6

From the wrinkle between my brows
You watch till day breaks
On my face

The waxen night
Is beginning to singe
The fingers of dawn

Black bricks
Have already tiled
The whole dome of the sky

7

Toothed eyes fly
Over still waters

Around us purple lips
Flutter from branches

Screams hit the blue
And fall onto pillows

Our homes hide
Behind narrow backs

Hands clutch at
Flimsy clouds

Our veins roll turbid
Beds and tables

Of shattered bones
Noon has fallen into our hands

And turned all gloomy

An open grave on the face of the earth
On your face on my face

8

At the crossroads
We meet the shadows
Blue beneath the eyes of day

If I turn my head
The sun will fall from the branch

You have buried smiles
In the palms of my hands
How can I bring them to life

My shadow keeps growing heavier
Someone is tying its wings

Goodness
You open your eyes you hide me dumbly
A sudden night is hunting me

At the end of the avenue
A plane tree lights a cigarette

9

Venomous green
Moments go marching
Across our foreheads

We travel out of our bodies
In a silence drawn
By our crazed glances

Between my eyelids
I hug your naked glance
To crush the pain in it

10

How with these buttons of bronze
Can we see

The darkness mocks us
Whips us with its hair

How with these paper tongues
Can we speak

Our words set light to them
Dry under the roofs of our mouths

How with these bodies of quicksand
Can we survive

Unbridled spoons
Carry us away grain by grain

How with these leafless wooden arms
Can we embrace

The carnations perish from our lips
Perish in the hot sand

11

The houses have turned out
The rooms' bitter pockets
For the whirlwind to search

Along our ribs
The street-lamps
Take off their bloodstained frocks

We are two sheets of newspaper
Crudely pasted
Over the evening's wound

Flaming birds
From my eyebrows
Have dropped onto your collarbones

12

Murky passages flow
From our eyelashes down our faces

With a fierce red-hot wire
Anger hems up our thoughts

Scissors with raised hackles
Around our unarmed words

The venomous rain of eternity
Bites us greedily

13

The pillars supporting heaven crumble

The bench with us slowly
Falls into the void

Must we forever languish
In stone silence

Through our eyes through our foreheads
Our words will sprout

The days have scattered

Must we forever wait for the sun
To show yellow through our ribs

We hear our hearts beating
In the throats of the dead pillars

We have fled out of our breasts

14

If it were not for your eyes
There would be no sky
In our blind dwelling

If it were not for your laughter
The walls would never
Vanish from our eyes

If it were not for your nightingales
The tender willows would never
Step over the threshold

If it were not for your arms
The sun would never
Spend the night in our sleep

15

The streets of your glances
Have no ending

The swallows from your eyes
Do not migrate south

From the aspens in your breasts
The leaves do not fall

In the sky of your words
The sun does not set

16

You put a decent light on
In my brown study

You spread me a meadow
On your breasts

You gather doves
White in my joy

You stub the cigarette of my worries
In your heart

In a bunch of muscats
You wait for my lips

17

I would sleep in the sea
I dive in the pupils of your eyes

I would blossom on the pavement
I trace flowerbeds in your walk

I would wake up in heaven
I make my bed in your laughter

I would play invisible
I lock myself in your heart

I would steal you from silence
I dress you in song

18

I carry you
A day rich in my arms
I plant
A line of firs along my gaze

I roam
The cities of your silences

I gather
The dew from your eyelashes

I break
A slender night across your waist

I call
Anxious dawns down from the roofs

19

Our youth is in leaf
Green down every street

The cheeks of houses glow
As we pass

The pavements play cards
With our feet

We are a sudden star
On the faces of passers-by

Flocks of surprises
Peck from our hands

20

Birds drink living water
Bubbling from your palms

Blue and brown birds
Which fly up from our eyes
When there's no hunter for miles

Your palms light up
Over two imagined lumps of earth
When the sun is late

21

Your hands glow on the hearth
In the middle of my face

Your hands open me the day

Your hands flower
In the faraway desert within me
Where no one has ever set foot

Your hands dream in mine
The dream of every starry hand on earth

22

Our day is a green apple
Cut in two

I look at you
You do not see me
Between us is the blind sun

On the steps
Our torn embrace

You call me
I do not hear you
Between us is the deaf air

In shop windows
My lips are seeking
Your smile

At the crossroads
Our trampled kiss

I have given you my hand
You do not feel it
Emptiness has embraced you

In the squares
Your tear is seeking
My eyes

In the evening my day dead
Meets with your dead day

Only in sleep
Do we walk the same paths

23

Without your glances I am a river
Whose banks have left her

The wind leads me by the hand
Twilight has cut off your hands
White streets flee before me

And fingers shun my forehead
Where the world has caught flame

My words are overgrown with grass
Silence has blown away your voice
Things are turning their grey backs on me

In the dark of my body
An evil light is on the prowl

24

I go
From one hand to the other
Where are you

I would embrace you
I embrace your absence
I would kiss your voice
I hear the laughter of distances
My lips have torn my face

From my parched hands
Shining appear to me
I want to see you
And I close my eyes

I go
From one side of my head to the other
Where are you

25

I am the yellow floor
In the empty room you are sitting in
Just so your shadow will comfort me

And I am the wooden stairs
You take from the room to the street
Just so I can play with your shadow

I am the dry leaves
In the streets you walk down
So I can hear your shadow

And I am the bare rock by the road
You pass along
So your shadow can dress me

26

In this morningless night
Who is that light on the corner

It wraps me in your gaze
Follows me to our blinded flat
Shines on the empty levées of my veins

And who is that bird
In the cracked sky of my heart
The only bird

It calls me with your voice
For white cannot
Fly down to earth

27

Between my palms
I have warmed the street
You returned along

Your voice has left its whiteness
Behind on the rooftops

The hours I have been lonely with
Rise before you
From their snowy chair

28

Beneath your eyelids
Your violets sleep

I turn myself into a sun
Above your nightmare

You throw open
Every window in your forehead

I pick you white
Waterlilies from my blood

You give my tree of ashes
Green leaves

29

These are your lips
That I return
To your neck

This is my moonlight
That I take down
From your shoulders

We have lost each other
In the boundless forests
Of our meeting

In my hands
Your adam's apples
Set and dawn

In your throat
Flame up and fade
My impetuous stars

We have found each other
On the golden plateau
Far within us

30

I peel the dusk from my body
Day has found me a face
The wind has cheered up my hair

My dumbstruck gaze grows leaf
A shadow sprouts from the sun
The world waits on the threshold of the heart

I descend blue slopes again
And enter your clear voice
To fetch our magic lamp

[1943–1951]

UNREST-FIELD

Will I be able
On this unrest-field
To raise you a tent of my hands

FAR WITHIN US *(1943)*

BEFORE PLAY

for Zoran Mišić

You close one eye
You peer into yourself look in all the corners
Make sure there are no nails no thieves
No cuckoos' eggs

Then you close your other eye as well
You crouch then jump
You jump as high as high as high
Right up to the top of yourself

Then your own weight drags you down
You fall for days as deep as deep as deep
Down to the bottom of your abyss

If you're not smashed to bits
If you're still in one piece and get up in one piece
Then you can play

THE NAIL

One is the nail another the pincers
The rest are workmen

The pincers grip the nail by the head
Grip him with their teeth with their hands
And tug him tug
To get him out of the floor
Usually they only pull his head off
It's hard to get a nail out of a floor

Then the workmen say
The pincers are no good
They smash their jaws and break their arms
And throw them out of the window

After that someone else is the pincers
Someone else the nail
The rest are workmen

HIDE-AND-SEEK

Someone hides from someone
Hides under his tongue
He looks for him under the earth

He hides in his forehead
He looks for him in the sky

He hides in his forgetting
He looks for him in the grass

Looks for him looks
Where doesn't he look for him
And looking for him loses himself

THE SEDUCER

One fondles the leg of a chair
Until the chair turns
And gives him the glad with its leg

Another kisses a keyhole
Kisses it doesn't he just kiss it
Until the keyhole returns the kiss

A third stands by
Gapes at the other two
And twists his head twists it

Until his head falls off

THE WEDDING

Each takes off his skin
Each uncovers his constellation
Which has never seen the night

Each fills his skin with stones
Each starts dancing with it
By the light of his own stars

He who doesn't stop until dawn
He who doesn't blink doesn't drop
He earns his skin

(This game is rarely played)

THE ROSE-THIEVES

Someone is a rose tree
Some are the wind's daughters
Some the rose-thieves

The rose-thieves creep up on the rose tree
One of them steals a rose
Hides it in his heart

The wind's daughters appear
See the tree stripped of its beauty
And give chase to the rose-thieves

Open up their breasts one by one
In some they find a heart
In some so help me none

They go on opening up their breasts
Until they uncover one heart
And in that heart the stolen rose

BETWEEN GAMES

No one is resting

This one keeps moving his eyes about
Puts them on his shoulders
And willy-nilly goes backwards
Puts them on the soles of his feet
And again willy-nilly comes back headlong

And this one has turned himself altogether into an ear
And heard everything that's not to be heard
But he's had enough
And is aching to turn back into himself
But without eyes he can't see how

And that one has uncovered all his faces
And is chasing them one after the other over the roofs
The last he throws underfoot
And buries his head in his hands

And this one has stretched out his glance
Stretched it from thumb to thumb
And is walking along it walking
At first slowly then more quickly
And quicker and quicker

And that one is playing with his head
Tosses it up in the air
And catches it on his forefinger
Or doesn't catch it at all

No one is resting

HE

Some bite off the others'
Arm or leg or whatever

Take it between their teeth
Run off as quick as they can
Bury it in the earth

The others run in all directions
Sniff search sniff search
Turn up all the earth

If any are lucky enough to find their arm
Or leg or whatever
It's their turn to bite

The game goes on briskly

As long as there are arms
As long as there are legs
As long as there is anything whatever

THE SEED

Someone sows someone
Sows him in his head
Stamps the earth down well

Waits for the seed to sprout

The seed hollows out his head
Turns it into a mousehole
The mice eat the seed

They drop dead

The wind comes to live in the empty head
And gives birth to chequered breezes

LEAPFROG

One is a stone on another's heart
A house-heavy stone
Neither under the stone can budge

And both struggle
At least to lift a finger
At least to click their tongue at least to move their ears
Or at least to blink

Neither under the stone can budge

And both struggle
And exhaust themselves and fall asleep from exhaustion
And it's only in their sleep their hair stands on end

(This game lasts a long time)

THE HUNTER

Someone goes in without knocking
Goes into somebody's one ear
And comes out of the other

Goes in with the step of a match
The step of a lighted match
Dances round inside his head

He's made it

Someone goes in without knocking
Goes into somebody's one ear
And doesn't come out of the other

He's done for

ASHES

Some are nights others stars

Each night lights up its star
And dances a black dance round it
Until the star burns out

Then the nights split up
Some become stars
The others remain nights

Again each night lights up its star
And dances a black dance round it
Until the star burns out

The last night becomes both star and night
It lights itself
Dances the black dance round itself

AFTER PLAY

At last the hands clasp the belly
Lest the belly burst with laughing
But the belly's not there

One hand just manages to lift itself
To wipe the cold sweat from the forehead
The forehead's gone too

The other hand clutches at the heart
Lest the heart leap out of the breast
The heart's gone too

Both hands drop
Idle drop into the lap
The lap's gone too

On one hand now the rain is falling
From the other grass is growing
What more should I say

[1954]

Bone to Bone

I / AT THE BEGINNING

That's better
We've got away from the flesh

Now we will do what we will
Say something

Would you like to be
The backbone of a streak of lightning

Say something more

What should I say to you
Pelvis of a storm

Say something else

I know nothing else
Ribs of the sky

We're no one's bones
Say something different

II / AFTER THE BEGINNING

What'll we do now

Yes what'll we do
Now we'll have marrow for supper

We ate the marrow for lunch
Now I've got a hollow grumbling

Then we'll make music
We like music

What'll we do when the dogs come
They like bones

Then we'll stick in their throats
And have fun

III / IN THE SUN

It's marvellous sunbathing naked
I couldn't stand the flesh

I wasn't keen on those rags either
I'm crazy about you naked like this

Don't let the sun caress you
Let's love each other just the two of us

Only not here only not in the sun
Here everything can be seen bone darling

IV / UNDERGROUND

Muscle of darkness muscle of flesh
It comes to the same thing

Well what shall we do now

We'll invite all the bones of all times
We'll bake in the sun

What shall we do then

Then we'll grow pure
Go on growing as we please

What shall we do afterwards

Nothing we'll wander here and there
We'll be eternal beings of bone

Just wait for the earth to yawn

V / IN THE MOONLIGHT

What's that now
As if flesh some snowy flesh
Were clinging to me

I don't know what it is
As if marrow were running through me
Some cold marrow

I don't know either
As if everything were beginning again
With a more horrible beginning

Do you know what
Can you bark

VI / BEFORE THE END

Where shall we go now

Where should we go nowhere
Where else would two bones go

What shall we do there

There long awaiting us
There eagerly expecting us
No one and his wife nothing

What use are we to them

They are old they are without bones
We'll be just like daughters to them

VII / AT THE END

I am a bone you are a bone
Why have you swallowed me
I can't see myself any more

What's wrong with you
It's you who've swallowed me
I can't see myself either

Where am I now

Now no one knows any more
Who is where nor who is who
All is an ugly dream of dust

Can you hear me

I can hear both you and myself
There's cockspur crowing out of us

[1956]

Give Me Back My Rags

Just come to my mind
My thoughts will scratch out your face

Just come into my sight
My eyes will start snarling at you

Just open your mouth
My silence will smash your jaws

Just remind me of you
My remembering will paw up the ground under your feet

That's what it's come to between us

1

Give me back my rags

My rags of pure dreaming
Of silk smiling of striped foreboding
Of my cloth of lace

My rags of spotted hope
Of burnished desire of chequered glances
Of skin from my face

Give me back my rags
Give me when I ask you nicely

2

Listen you monster
Take off that white scarf
We know each other

Since we were so high
Guzzled from the same bowl

Slept in the same bed
With you evil-eyed knife

Roamed the crooked world
With you snake in the grass

Do you hear dissembler
Take off that white scarf
Why lie to each other

3

I won't carry you pick-a-back
I won't take you wherever you say

I won't not even shod with gold
Nor harnessed to the wind's three-wheeled chariot
Nor bridled with the rainbow's bridle

You can't buy me

I won't not even with my feet in my pocket
Nor threaded through a needle nor tied in a knot
Nor reduced to an ordinary rod

You can't scare me

I won't not even distilled or double-distilled
Nor raw nor salted
I won't not even in a dream

Don't kid yourself
It's not on I won't

4

Get out of my walled infinity
Of the star circle round my heart
Of my mouthful of sun

Get out of the comic sea of my blood
Of my flow of my ebb
Get out of my stranded silence

Get out I said get out

Get out of my living abyss
Of the bare father-tree within me

Get out how long must I cry get out

Get out of my bursting head
Get out just get out

5

You get harebrained puppets

And I bath them in my blood
Dress them in rags of my skin

I make them swings of my hair
Prams of my vertebrae
Kites of my eyebrows

I shape them butterflies of my smiles
And wild beasts of my teeth
For them to hunt to kill time

A fine sort of game that is

6

Damn your root and blood and crown
And everything in life

The thirsty pictures in your brain
The fire-eyes on your fingertips
And every every step

To three cauldrons of cross-grained water
Three furnaces of symbol fire
Three nameless milkless pits

Damn your cold breath down your gullet
To the stone under your left breast
To the cut-throat bird in that stone

To the crow of crows the nest of emptiness
The hungry shears of beginning and beginning
To heaven's womb don't I know it

Damn your seed and sap and shine
And dark and stop at the end of my life
And everything in the world

7

What about my rags
Won't you give them back won't you

I'll burn your eyebrows
You won't be invisible to me for ever

I'll mix day and night in your mind
You'll come beating your head on my door

I'll cut off your singing nails
So you can't draw hopscotch through my brain

I'll hound the fogs out of your bones
So they drink the hemlock off your tongue

You'll see what I'll do to you

8

And you want us to love one another

You can shape me from my ashes
From the débris of my guffawing
From my leftover tedium

You can gorgeous

You can seize me by the hair of forgetting
Embrace my night in an empty shirt
Kiss my echo

Well you don't know how to love

9

Flee monster

Even our footsteps bite each other
Bite behind us in the dust
We're not meant for each other

Rock-fast cold I look through you
I pass through you from end to end
This is no game

Why ever did we mix the rags up

Give them back what do you want them for
There's no use their fading on your back
Give them back flee into your nowhere land

Monster flee from the monster

Where are your eyes
Over here there's a monster too

10

Black be your tongue black your noon black your hope
All be black only my horror white
My wolf be at your throat

The storm be your bed
My dread your pillow
Broad your unrest-field

Your food of fire your teeth of wax
Now chew you glutton
Chew all you want

Dumb be your wind dumb water dumb flowers
All be dumb only my gnashing aloud
My hawk be at your heart

Terror your mother be bereft

11

I've wiped your face off my face
Ripped your shadow off my shadow

Levelled the hills in you
Turned your plains into hills

Set your seasons quarrelling
Turned all the ends of the world from you

Wrapped the path of my life around you
My impenetrable my impossible path

Just try to meet me now

12

Enough chattering violets enough sweet trash
I won't hear anything know anything
Enough enough of all

I'll say the last enough
Fill my mouth with earth
Grit my teeth

To break off you skull-guzzler
To break off once for all

I'll be just what I am
Without root without branch without crown
I'll lean on myself
On my own bumps and bruises

I'll be the hawthorn stake through you
That's all I can be in you
In you spoilsport in you muddlehead

Get lost

13

Don't try your tricks monster

You hid a knife under your scarf
You stepped over the line you tripped me up
You spoiled the game

So my heaven might overturn
The sun smash my head
My rags be scattered

Monster don't try your tricks with the monster

Give me back my rags
I'll give you yours

The Quartz Pebble

QUARTZ PEBBLE

>*for Dušan Radić*

Headless limbless
It appears
With the excitable pulse of chance
It moves
With the shameless march of time
It holds all
In its passionate
Internal embrace

A smooth white innocent torso
It smiles with the eyebrow of the moon

THE HEART OF THE QUARTZ PEBBLE

They played with the pebble
The stone like any other stone
Played with them as if it had no heart

They got angry with the pebble
Smashed it in the grass
Puzzled they saw its heart

They opened the pebble's heart
In the heart a snake
A sleeping coil without dreams

They roused the snake
The snake shot up into the heights
They ran off far away

They looked from afar
The snake coiled round the horizon
Swallowed it like an egg

They came back to the place of their game
No trace of snake or grass or bits of pebble
Nothing anywhere far around

They looked at each other they smiled
And they winked at each other

THE DREAM OF THE QUARTZ PEBBLE

A hand appeared out of the earth
Flung the pebble into the air

Where is the pebble
It hasn't come back to earth
It hasn't climbed up to heaven

What's become of the pebble
Have the heights devoured it
Has it turned into a bird

Here is the pebble
Stubborn it has stayed in itself
Not in heaven nor in earth

It obeys itself
Among the worlds a world

THE LOVE OF THE QUARTZ PEBBLE

He fell for a beautiful
A rounded blue-eyed
A frivolous endlessness

He is quite transformed
Into the white of her eye

Only she understands him
Only her embrace has
The shape of his desire
Dumb and boundless

All her shadows
He has captured in himself

He is blind in his love
And he sees
No other beauty
But her whom he loves
And who will cost him his head

THE ADVENTURE OF THE QUARTZ PEBBLE

He's had enough of the circle
The perfect circle around him
He's stopped short

His load is heavy
His own load inside him
He's dropped it

His stone is hard
The stone he's made of
He's left it

He's cramped in himself
In his own body
He's come out

He's hidden from himself
Hidden in his own shadow

THE SECRET OF THE QUARTZ PEBBLE

He's filled himself with himself
Has he eaten too much of his own tough flesh
Does he feel ill

Ask him don't be afraid
He's not begging for bread

He's petrified in a blissful convulsion
Is he pregnant perhaps
Will he give birth to a stone
Or a wild beast or a streak of lightning

Ask him as much as you like
Don't expect an answer

Expect only a bump
Or a second nose or a third eye
Or who knows what

TWO QUARTZ PEBBLES

They look at each other dully
Two pebbles look at each other

Two sweets yesterday
On the tongue of eternity
Two stone tears today
On an eyelash of the unknown

Two flies of sand tomorrow
In the ears of deafness
Two merry dimples tomorrow
In the cheeks of day

Two victims of a little joke
A bad joke without a joker

They look at each other dully
With cold cruppers they look at each other
They talk without lips
They talk hot air

[1951–1954]

SECONDARY HEAVEN

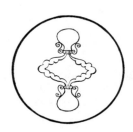

THE STAR-GAZER'S LEGACY

His words remained after him
Fairer than the world
No one dares gaze at them

They wait at time's turnings
Greater than people
Can anyone pronounce them

They lie on the dumb earth
Heavier than life's bones
Death didn't manage
To carry them off as a dowry

No one can lift them up
No one can throw them down

The falling stars hide their heads
In the shadows of his words

A FORGETFUL NUMBER

Once upon a time there was a number
Pure and round like the sun
But alone very much alone

It began to reckon with itself

It divided multiplied itself
It subtracted added itself
And remained always alone

It stopped reckoning with itself
And shut itself up in its round
And sunny purity

Outside were left the fiery
Traces of its reckoning

They began to chase each other through the dark
To divide when they should have multiplied themselves
To subtract when they should have added themselves

That's what happens in the dark

And there was no one to ask it
To stop the traces
And to rub them out

A CONCEITED MISTAKE

Once upon a time there was a mistake
So silly so small
That no one would even have noticed it

It couldn't bear
To see itself to hear of itself

It invented all manner of things
Just to prove
That it didn't really exist

It invented space
To put its proofs in
And time to keep its proofs
And the world to see its proofs

All it invented
Was not so silly
Nor so small
But was of course mistaken

Could it have been otherwise

A WISE TRIANGLE

Once upon a time there was a triangle
It had three sides
The fourth it hid
In its glowing centre

By day it would climb to its three vertices
And admire its centre
By night it would rest
In one of its three angles

At dawn it would watch its three sides
Transformed into three glowing wheels
Disappear into the blue of no return

It would take out its fourth side
Kiss it break it three times
And hide it once more in its former place

And again it had three sides

And again by day it would climb
To its three vertices
And admire its centre
And by night it would rest
In one of its three angles

PETRIFIED ECHOES

Once upon a time there was an infinity of echoes
They served one voice
Built it arcades

The arcades collapsed
They'd built them crooked
The dust covered them

They left the dangerous service
Became petrified from hunger

They flew off petrified
To find to tear to pieces the mouth
The voice had come out of

They flew who knows how long
And blind fools didn't see
They were flying round the very edge of the mouth
They were looking for

THE STORY OF A STORY

Once upon a time there was a story

It ended
Before its beginning
And it began
After its end

Its heroes entered it
After their death
And left it
Before their birth

Its heroes talked
About some earth about some heaven
They said all sorts of things

The only thing they didn't say
Was what they didn't know
That they are only heroes in a story

In a story that ends
Before its beginning
And that begins
After its end

YAWN OF YAWNS

Once upon a time there was a yawn
Not under the palate not under the hat
Not in the mouth not in anything

It was bigger than everything
Bigger than its own bigness

From time to time
Its darkness dull desperate darkness
In desperation would flash here and there
You might think it was stars

Once upon a time there was a yawn
Boring like any yawn
And still it seems it lasts

AN INTRUDER

A drop of blood in the corner of heaven

Have the stars perhaps begun
To divide the blue again to bite each other
Or kiss each other

At the sun's round table
Nothing is said about it

Only the fiery bread is broken
Beakers of light pass from hand to hand
And dead stars gnaw their own bones

What does the drop of blood want in the corner of
heaven
In that one-eyed corner of heaven

A WINGED PIPE

A winged pipe flies around
The streaks of lightning in a vast coil
With a song it tries to lure them somewhere

Is it back to the clouds
Or to another lovelier heaven
Or to earth among men

It's tangled in the tongues of flame
Song and wings are burning
And its shadow on the gates of heaven

Doesn't it know some other song

This one will only enrage the lightning streaks
Not lure them anywhere

AN OBSTINATE BUNDLE

A formless white bundle
Moves over the clear heaven

Constantly with all its strength it rocks from side to side
Tied crosswise with green string
And so prepares its step

Constantly struggling it falls
On to the uncaring soil of heaven
And so marks time

Above it one star keeps silence

Below it another star keeps silence
To its right an old sun philosophizes
To its left a young moon raves

Why doesn't it just calm down for once
The good-natured thunder from the clear heaven
Will certainly untie it

A HOMELESS HEAD

A severed head
A head with a flower in its teeth
Wandering circles the earth

The sun meets it
It bows to him
And continues its journey

The moon meets it
To him it smiles
And doesn't break its journey

Why does it growl at the earth
Can't it return
Or leave for ever

Its flowering lips would know

A CONDEMNED DAGGER

A naked grey-eyed dagger
Lies on the Milky Way

How it wriggles
In the star dust
Is it thirsty for blood

How it leaps up
Does it want to stab
Its own innocent shadow

And how it flashes its blades
Flashes on all sides
Is it signalling to someone

The processions of stars avoid it
And leave an empty space
In the shape of a heart around it

Where's the world-famous hand
That flung it up there
It's time it took it back again

BURNING HANDS

Two burning hands are drowning
In the depths of heaven

They don't grasp at the star
That is floating around them
And blinking and crossing itself

They're saying something with their fingers
Who can decipher
The tongue of fingers in the flame

Solemnly they put their palms together
The sign of a roof top

Are they talking of the old house
They left burnt down
Or perhaps of the new one
They're just thinking of building

THE LAST ROPE

A fat gaudy rope
Crawls between the constellations
And can scarcely get through

At each starry crossroads
It ties itself a knot
To remember all the paths

Its endless end
It ceaselessly draws
Out of the blue womb of heaven

It crawls between the constellations
Towards the very heart of the world
And never gets tangled

A CROWNED APPLE

Take the sun out of your mouth
Night is burying us alive

This is my apple
It fell on my tongue from heaven
Leave me alone to savour it

Open your mouth zero so dawn may come to us
So the sun may crown us too

Pray that I do not open my mouth
There are no more sweet jobs in the apple
For you maggots

A BLUE NOOSE

Why do you squeeze our necks with the horizon

I like to have the pleats of heaven
Fall thickly over my thighs

You'll throttle us with that belt

I like your lament for the blue noose
When I am tired and unbelt myself

A HIGH PATH

Pick up your big foot
You're treading on our thought

I cannot carry my steps
Through you in my arms

Move off our thought
Will bite the stars off the soles of your feet

I cannot sacrifice my path
It leads me through your heads

HARDWORKING THREADS

Why do your glances
Stitch up our eyelids

I don't know what the sunbeams
Are doing behind my back

Why don't you turn your head
To see your glances

Now I don't know where my head is
If you need it you find it

FOSTER BROOD

Gather up your thunderbolts
They're hatching under our hearts

Why don't you cherish
The echoes of my words yourselves

Gather them up they'll smash both us
And you to smithereens

Why don't you come on their tail
And fly into my heart

FERTILE FIRE

Cut yourself lengthwise zero
That we too may stand upright

Have you really grown so much
Playing on my fire

Cut yourself crosswise zero
That we too may spread our arms

Are you really prepared to fly up
By yourselves to the source of my fire

FREE FLIGHT

Give us leave to fly away
Out of your palace without foundation

I've forged you into stars
Under the vault of my skull
Fly away who's stopping you

Give us leave to perish
Each flight brings us back to the palace

Got you there my birds
Cut off your wings
So your flight will be free

DEATH OF THE SUN'S FATHER

Three paces from the top of heaven
From the limetree in eternal bloom
The old sun stopped

Turned red turned green
Turned round himself three times
And went back to his rising

(So as not to die in our sight)

They say there's a Son of the Sun
Until he's born wide-eyed for us too
We'll teach this darkness to shine

BLIND SUN

Two lame sunbeams
Lead the blind sun

Morning is seeking his fortune
On the other side of heaven
He's not on his own doorstep

Midday has fallen low
He's gadding about with the lightning
He's never at home

Evening has gone out into the world
With his bedding on his back
He's begging on some star

With open arms
Only night has come out
To meet the blind sun

CLASH AT THE ZENITH

A blue sun was born
In heaven's left armpit
A black sun was born
In heaven's right armpit

The blue one climbs the black one climbs
Towards the tower in the zenith
Where desolation now resides

We have gone down naked into ourselves

We open up the molehills
We whisper the secret name
Of our own native sun

The golden tripod from the tower
Has set out in three directions

PREPARATIONS FOR A WELCOME

We set up a gate
Of our flowering bones
At the entrance to heaven

We spread half our soul
Up one slope of heaven

We think up a table
Of our petrified hands
At the very top of heaven

We spread half our soul
Down the other slope of heaven

We build a bed
Of our leafy heart
At the way out of heaven

We do all this in the dark
Alone without the help of time

We wonder if these are really
Preparations for a welcome
Or only a farewell

MIDNIGHT SUN

From a huge black egg
A sun was hatched to us

It shone on our ribs
It opened heaven wide
In our wretched breasts

It didn't set at all
But it didn't rise either

It turned everything in us gold
It turned nothing green
Around us around that gold

It changed into a tombstone
On our living heart

FOREIGN SUN

Whose head did this one-eyed bastard
Drop out of

Who's he gawping at now
Who's he rolling after
Over the fallow heavens

Why is he sizing us up
He'd just love to burn us to cinders

As if from down here we
Had doused his rabid father
With cold water

He'd better cool off
He's got the wrong heaven

IMITATION OF THE SUN

The heart of one of us rose
High into the burnt-out heaven

It moved off along the sun's path
Overgrown with iron weeds
And it set behind the charred horizon

We waited in vain for it to return
With the young apple-bearer
Or at least with twelve fiery branches

Since then we all carry
Our hearts on a heavy chain
Fastened to a faithful rib

GLUTTONOUS SMOKE

Why did you abandon me
As the smoke bore me upwards

It was you abandoned us at the bottom
Of your emptied lower cauldron

Why didn't you look for me
As the same smoke bore me downwards

It's for you to look for us now on the rim
Of your overturned upper cauldron

Why didn't you call to me
As the smoke swallowed me alive

It's for you to call to us now through the ears
Of both lower and upper cauldrons

A CAKE OF ASHES

Are you still keeping my fire
That I left you

You left us
A stale cake of ashes

Have you unlocked the sign
Of my gate on the crust

We have unlocked the sign
Of your crossed daggers

Are you eating the golden
Sunflower hidden within it

Your cake has eaten our hands
As we were breaking it

AN EXTINGUISHED WHEEL

Where were you going so happily
With my fiery wheel of thought

We turned on the spot
With it extinguished round our neck

Where did you get to so happily
With my poor blind wheel

Carried away we drove it
To overtake itself

Where did you vanish to
With my demented wheel

Angry we pulled it off our neck
Together with our head

A FIREPROOF SPOOL

Are you still hanging headless
By one of my black rays

We are hanging in your ancient smoke
By one of our golden threads

Do you still not know in the dark
That my ray has burnt out

We know that the faithful thread
Has unwound from our heart

Do you still not see in the dark
That my ray has snapped

We see that our thread is searching
High above the heart for its spool

A CLOT OF DARKNESS

Do you not recognize the clot
Of my ancient curdled darkness

We are cutting to pieces before it
Innocent gold-haired remembering

Do you not yearn for its secret
By which it would illuminate you

We are chasing forgetting around it
To bite its own tail

Do you not grasp its circles
Above your empty shoulders

We are afraid lest your clot
Replace our lost head

THE FIERY SUNFLOWER

Whence comes at the top of your spine
The dancing circles of fiery tongues

We were playing tunes on our shinbones
It formed of itself

Whence comes in the midst of your circle
The scorched many-eyed field

We were slapping our thighs
It began to glow hot of itself

Whence comes your hidden sunflower
Whole unbroken uneaten

We found it on our shoulders
In place of our red-hot head

AN INCANDESCENT KISS

What are you doing without my blue glory
In your soft tower tending to its fall

We're setting fire to our last breath
Above the mouth of your lower cauldron

What are you starting without my start
Behind your bone bars

We're setting fire to our first loneliness
Below the mouth of your upper cauldron

What are you ending without my end
Behind your chirping bolt

We're dreaming that from the incandescent kiss
We save ourselves the cauldron's ears

THE SONG OF YOUNG TRUTH

Truth sang in the darkness
On top of the limetree in the heart

The sun it said will ripen
On top of the limetree in the heart
If the eyes shine on it

We mocked the song
Seized and bound truth
And murdered it here under the limetree

The eyes were busy
Outside in another darkness
And saw nothing

A DRAGON IN THE WOMB

A fiery dragon in the womb
In the dragon a red cave
In the cave a white lamb
In the lamb the old heaven

We fed the dragon with earth
We wanted to tame it
And steal the old heaven

We were left without earth
We didn't know where to go next
We mounted the dragon's tail

The dragon looked at us furiously
We took fright at our own face
In the dragon's eyes

We jumped into the dragon's jaws
Crouched behind his teeth
And waited for the fire to save us

THE TAMING OF THE DAGGER

For a long time a dagger hung
Squinting above our heart

The severed wings flew up
Out of the limetree in the heart
And tamed the dagger

The wings taught the dagger
In flight to trace
The young sun's face around the heart

The wings took the dagger
Utterly broken by its lesson
Somewhere high up in the dark

We bowed low
To the limetree in the heart

A FISH IN THE SOUL

A silver fish in the soul
In the fish a little straw
On the straw a gaudy cloth
On the cloth three virgin stars

We caught the silver fish
We were really hungry
The fish scarcely tried to escape

We opened the fish up
Out of the fish spilt a little straw

The gaudy cloth fell apart
And the three virgin stars
Lost their virginity

As for the silver fish
Even the cats wouldn't eat it
It was a big disappointment

It is dark now in our soul

THE SUFFERING OF THE GOLDEN STOOL

A golden stool limped
Around our hidden heart
And with its leg dug the darkness

We were afraid it might dig
Under the limetree in the heart

It was certainly trying to dig up someone
Who had already sat on it
Or someone who would yet sit on it

It limped around the buried secret
Counted over its three legs
And dug itself out three graves

We danced the sun dance
Around the limetree in the heart

A DOVE IN THE HEAD

A transparent dove in the head
In the dove a clay coffer
In the coffer a dead sea
In the sea a blessed moon

We split open the dove
Smashed the clay coffer
Spilt the dead sea

We waded into the sea
Got to the bottom

Deep below the bottom
We saw the transparent dove
And in it a young moon

We came to the surface

High above the surface
Again we saw the dove
And in it a full moon

We began to drink the dead sea

THE LIMETREE IN THE HEART

A flowering limetree in the heart
Beneath the limetree a buried cauldron
In the cauldron twelve clouds
In the clouds a young sun

We dug for the cauldron through the heart
Dug out the twelve clouds
The cauldron fled with the sun
From one depth to another

We gaped into the last depth
Deeper than our own life
We threw up the digging

We cut down the limetree to warm ourselves
Our heart was cold

THE STAR-GAZER'S DEATH

He had to die they say
The stars were closer to him
Even than people

He was eaten they say by ants
He imagined that stars
Gave birth to ants and ants to stars
So he filled the house with ants

His heavenly trollops they say
Did him in
And the rumours are absurd of a dagger
With human fingerprints

He was simply out of this world they say
He had gone to find the sunflower
In which meet the paths
Of every heart and every star

He had to die they say

HEAVEN'S RING

Ring no one's ring
How did you get lost
How fall from heaven somewhere
Rather everywhere than somewhere

Why did you marry so soon
Your old your ancient shine
To your young emptiness

They have forgotten both you
And their wedding night

Since then your shine has taken to drink
Your emptiness has run to fat
You are lost again

Here is my ring-finger
Settle down on it

NOTHINGNESS

Nothingness you were asleep
And dreamt that you were something

Something caught fire
The flame writhed
In blind agonies

You woke up nothingness
And warmed your back
At the dream flame

You didn't see the flame's agonies
Whole worlds of agonies
Your back is short-sighted

Nothingness you fell asleep again
And dreamt that you were nothing

The flame went out
Its agonies received their sight
And they too went out in bliss

ORPHAN ABSENCE

You had no proper father
Your mother wasn't at home
When you saw the world in yourself
You were born by mistake

You have the figure of an abandoned abyss
There's a smell of absence about you
You gave birth to yourself

You run around with fiery sluts
You break your heads one after the other
Jump out of one of your mouths into another
And rejuvenate the old mistake

Stoop naked if you can
To my last letter
And follow its track

I have an idea orphan-child
That it leads to a sort of presence

THE SHADOW MAKER

You walk through a whole eternity
Along your personal infinity
From head to heels and back

You shine on yourself
In your head is the zenith
In your heels the setting of your shining

Before the setting you let your shadows
Stretch move away
Work miracles and shame
And bow to themselves

At the zenith you cut the shadows down
To their proper size
You teach them to bow to you
And as they bow they disappear

You're walking towards us even today
But you can't be seen for shadows

THE STARRY SNAIL

You crawled out after the rain
After the starry rain

The stars of their bones
Built you your house themselves
Where are you carrying it on the towel

Lame time is coming after you
To catch you up to tread on you
Put out your horns snail

You crawl over the vast cheek
Which you will never survey
Straight into the maw of nothingness

Turn aside to the life-line
On my dreamed hand
Before it is too late

And bequeath to me
The wonder-working towel of silver

FUGITIVE STARS

You looked at each other stars
Stealthily so heaven wouldn't see
You meant well

You were misunderstood

Dawn found you cold
Far from your hearth
Far from the gate of heaven

Look at me stars
Stealthily so earth won't see
Give me secret signs
I will give you a cherrywood staff

And one of my wrinkles as path
And one of my lashes as guide
To bring you home

[1962–1968]

EARTH ERECT

PILGRIMAGE

I walk with my father's staff in my hand
A burning heart on my staff

My footsteps spell out the letters
The holy road writes down for me

I draw them in the sand with my staff
Before sleep
At every hostelry

Lest they be wiped from my memory

I am still far from deciphering them
Right now they resemble
The constellation of the Wolf

I'll have something to fill my nights with
If I get back home safe and sound

CHELANDARION

O black Three-Handed Mother

Reach out one hand to me
Let me bathe in the magic ocean
Reach out a second hand
Let me eat my fill of the sweet stone

Reach out your third hand to me
Let me sleep in a nest of verses

I've come in from the road
Dusty and famished
Longing for a different world

Reach out three small tendernesses
Before a thousand mists fall on my eyes
And I lose my head

And before they cut off all your hands
O black Three-Handed Mother

KALENIĆ

Whence my eyes
In your face
Angel my brother

The colours dawn
On the edge of forgetting

Stranger-shades forbid me
To return the lightning
Of your sword to its sheath

The colours ripen
On the weightless branch of time

Hence your lovely stubbornness
At the corners of my mouth
Angel my brother

The colours burn
With youth in my blood

ŽIČA

O crimson lady Žiča
You issue from my heart

You stride seven-gated
Escorted by the sun your bridegroom
Over the ripe waves of corn

And stand at the very top
Of your chosen fiery triangle

You defy the sun-slayer
And the corn-defiler
From the two imperial corners below you

You stride toward your heights
And high love
In the only possible direction

Stride on I kiss your steps
O crimson lady Žiča

SOPOĆANI

Rosy calm of strength
Mature calm of greatness

From the golden birds below the earth
To the profusion of fruit in the heavens
All is within reach

The forms have knelt marvellously
In the artist's eye

(Time has gnawed)

Young beauty of pride
Sleepwalker certainty

The gates of eternal spring
And the bright weapons of happiness
All wait only for a sign

In the artist's right hand
Beat the pulses of the world

(Time has gnawed
And broken his teeth)

MANASIJA

Blue and gold
Last ring of the horizon
Last apple of the sun

O painter
How far can you see

Do you hear the night horsemen
Allah il ilallah

Your brush does not tremble
Your colours are not afraid

The night horsemen come closer
Allah il ilallah

O painter
What do you see in the night's depths

Gold and blue
Last star in the soul
Last infinity in the eye

SZENTENDRE

You fled to the end of eternity
Took seven more steps
Towards the north

You took out of the river of paradise
The skull of your namesake saint
And on its top you built
Seven sun shrines

Beneath the dome you set on fire
Seven old-men oaks
And anointed them with wine

From the fire you freed seven turtle-doves
With them sang seven vespers

You smelt an iris flower
Locked yourself in heaven's corona
And fell silent

[1950–1971]

In vain I went a pilgrim
To St Sava's spring

(Serbian Folk Song)

ST SAVA'S SPRING

Clear eye in the stone
Opened for always
By the staff's fourfold kiss

With sleepy green eyelashes
The grass both hides and uncovers
The cold transparent truth

At the bottom of this water
Shines the crystal wolf-head
With a rainbow in its jaws

To wash in this water
Heals all pain of death
To drink of this water
All pain of life

Clear eye in the stone
Open for all
Who leave their black tear-drop here

THE LIFE OF ST SAVA

Hungry and thirsty for holiness
He left the world
His own people and himself

He entered the service
Of the winged lords

He tended their golden-fleeced clouds
And groomed their thunder and lightning
Hobbled in the great tomes

He spent all his years
Earned a serpent-headed staff

He mounted the staff
Returned to the world
And found there his own people and himself

He lives without years without death
Surrounded by his wolves

ST SAVA

Around his head fly bees
And form a living halo

In his red beard
Strewn with lime flowers
Thunder and lightning play hide-and-seek

Round his neck hang chains
And twitch in their iron sleep

On his shoulder his cock blazes
In his hand his all-wise staff sings
A song of crossroads

To his left flows time
To his right flows time

He strides over dry land
Escorted by his wolves

ST SAVA'S PASTORAL WORK

He tends his white stone flock
On the green hillside

He helps each stone
In the inherited red cave
To give birth

Wherever he goes
His flock follows
The hills echo with stone footfalls

He stops in a yellow
Unapproachable glade
Milks the stones one by one

He gives the thirsty wolves
Thick stone milk to drink
Shimmering with the seven colours of the rainbow

Strong teeth and secret wings
Grow with the stone milk

ST SAVA'S FORGE

From the besieged hills
The wolves call him
Their backbones ablaze

He stretches out his serpent-headed staff
So they may crawl
Peacefully to his feet

He bathes them in the hot blood
Of the holy ancestral metal
And dries them with his red beard

He forges them new backbones
Of young iron
And sends them back to the hills

With endless howling
The wolves greet him
From the top of the liberated hills

ST SAVA'S SCHOOL

He sits at the top of a pear tree
Says something into his beard

He listens
The honey-lipped leaves
Are praying with his words

He watches
The wind the fire-bearer
Is cursing on the hills with his words

He smiles
And slowly he eats
The book of the lord of the world

And calls the hungry wolves

From the pear tree he throws them pages
Full of red long-necked letters
And white lambs

ST SAVA'S JOURNEY

He journeys over the dark land

With his staff he cuts
The dark beyond him into four

He flings thick gloves
Changed into immense cats
At the grey army of mice

Amid the storm he releases his chains
And lashes the ancient oaken land
To the fixed stars

He washes his wolves' paws
That no trace of the dark land
Should remain on them

He journeys without a path
And the path is born behind him

ST SAVA AT HIS SPRING

He looks
At his third eye in the stone

He sees in the impartial water
His pillaged coffin
Full of ripe big-bosomed pears

He sees his wolf-head
And on its brow the sign
Of the promised new constellation

He sees his flowering staff
And his land now happily fertile
In the flushed buds

He closes two eyes
And looks with the third eye in the stone

THE BLACKBIRD'S FIELD

A field like any other
A hand and a half of green

The young moon reaps
The migrant corn
Two crossed sunbeams
Build cruciform stooks

A blackbird reads aloud
The secret letters scattered over the field

Peonies high as heaven
Offer the four black winds
The warriors' united blood

A field like none other
Heaven above it
Heaven below

SUPPER ON THE BLACKBIRD'S FIELD

All sit at table transparent
And see the stars in each others' hearts

The crowned one breaks and shares out
Their golden past
And they eat it

He pours into their white peony goblets
Their ruby future
And they drink it

Across their knees under the table
Their swords are growling quietly

In the platters on the table
Is reflected the evening sky
And in the sky the end of tomorrow's battle

A blackbird flies down
On to the crowned one's right hand
And begins his song

THE BLACKBIRD'S SONG

I the blackbird
Among birds the black-cowled
Fold and unfold my wings

Perform the rites in my field
In my beak I transform
A dew-drop and a grain of earth into song

O battle tomorrow be fine
That is to say be just

O verdant Queen grass
Be victorious you alone

O victory make the Queen's servants rejoice
Who feed her with crimson milk

Make her star-servants rejoice also
Who clothe her in living silver

I sing
And I burn one feather from my left pinion
That my song may be accepted

THE BATTLE ON THE BLACKBIRD'S FIELD

Singing we ride over the field
To encounter the armoured dragons

Our most lovely wolf shepherd
His flowering staff in his hand
Flies through the air on his white steed

The crazed thirsty weapons
Savage each other alone in the field

From the mortally wounded iron
A river of our blood streams out
Flows upward and streams into the sun

The field stands up erect beneath us

We overtake the heavenly rider
And our betrothed stars
And together we fly through the blue

From below there follows
The blackbird's farewell song

THE CROWNED ONE OF THE BLACKBIRD'S FIELD

On his hand he holds his severed head
His bright shining benefaction
The sun's vice-regent
In the all-pervading dark

He stands beatific on a cloud
Barefoot in a torn shirt
Girt with the tail of a vanquished dragon

In a goblet brimful of blood
On his severed neck

The fragments of his sword become
Morsels of bread

Holy mother Saturday
Gives him second birth

He is alive in the crimson dew-drop
He dances in the burning circle of peonies
He sings in the blackbird's song on this field

THE WARRIORS OF THE BLACKBIRD'S FIELD

Where we are now
We are lords of the blue fields
And the ore-rich mountains with no foothills
We have married
Each his namesake star

Here in the kingdom we have won
Our arms crossed on our breasts
We continue the battle

We continue it backwards

We haven't yet reached
The start of the battle lads
God knows if we ever shall

From where we are we hear
Somewhere high above us
The blackbird's green song

THE BLACKBIRD'S MISSION

The blackbird dries his blood-drenched wings
At the fire of red peonies

Before him the field stretches out
Inscribed with molten human iron
Transmuted into honourable gold

Grass holds sway between the letters
And falls them into line
As it wills

The blackbird wrests his field
From the hands of the four black winds
And rolls it up from midday to midnight

At midnight he flies over the sky
Bears off in his beak somewhere he knows where
His green scroll

[1958–1971]

THE TOWER OF SKULLS

Tower of death

On the bony foreheads shimmers
A terrible memory

From the eye-sockets
Black clairvoyance looks
To the end of the world

Between the toothless jaws
Sticks
A monstrous last curse

Around death walled up in the tower
The skulls dance on the spot
The final starry dance

Tower of death
In it the châtelaine frightened
Of herself

INITIATION OF BLACK GEORGE

He doesn't yet know
Who he is

On his shoulders he's carrying the coffin
Of his holy king
From one tomb to another

The oaken planks whisper
And interpret at his ear
The language of the guiding stars

He listens frowning

He shifts the coffin
From one shoulder to the other
And crosses himself with his left hand

Future king of the paupers

BLACK GEORGE

From the stake my head is watching me
Come what may I'm dead and you are dead
Do you grasp it

Curse their souls and their sweet centres
Curse the horned moon on their brows
Curse the viper in their eyes
We'll not die

Towards the flowering key of existence
To the depths of a sea of curs' blood
No backward glance no future only follow me
Can you

Knives drawn curse all their earth and heaven
Death had its fill of us long since
Knives drawn my wolves the darlings of eternal pain

From the stakes your heads grin down at you
Come what may you're dead and I am dead
Will you

ROSE OVER ČEGAR

Is this our world or not

The blazing hawk drops from our faces
The wild boar leaves our hearts
Our nails clutch at our last breath

What else can we clutch at
No cloud will stretch out a hand
No stone offer a shoulder
Nor will time come to our aid
Who can count the teeth of death

No one O black blood still unspilt

Gnaw at the very heart of fear
Gnaw cloud and stone and time
And open a black rose in the air

Is this our world or not

DIRGE

They did not give you to the unbraided waters
They refused you to the bareheaded barrows
I wash your bones in blood
I wrap you in my eyelids

I plough my face it's all I have

You stepped over the threshold of heaven
I follow you red poppies with barefoot lips
My deserted flesh is maddened
It abandons me I abandon it

I smash my breasts what use are they to me

The fresh track of your teeth leads me
From rock to rock from star to star
Leads me from one circle into another

THE DEATH OF BLACK GEORGE

They cut off his head as he slept
Bore it away to the city of the king cur
And threw it to the whelps

When he wakes he'll go after it
A black handkerchief in his left hand
And a black rose in his right

His wolves will ride out to meet him
On black horses
With black banners

They'll carry his head
On crossed black flutes
Bound with widows' black braids

His head will shine
Crowned with black beams
Of the black sun

When he wakes

SONG OF THE TOWER OF SKULLS

to Svetozar Brkić

For the great-eyed sunflower you gave us
Blind stone your unface
And what now monster

You made us one with yourself
With the emptiness in your empty poison-tooth
With your dock-tailed eternity
Is that all your secret

Why now flee into our eye-sockets
Why hiss with darkness and sting with horror
Is that all you can do

That's not our teeth chattering it's the wind
Idle at the sun's fair
We grin at you grin up at heaven
What can you do to us

Our skulls are flowering with laughter
Look at us look your fill at yourself
We mock you monster

[1954–1971]

RETURN TO BELGRADE

This far to this cross of water
Three wolf-spoors have led me

I washed my face in the river of paradise
Dried it on the skirts of the Sun Mother
Bending over the steeples

I planted my father's staff
In the clay on the bank
To burst into leaf among the willows

I turned towards the great gate
Open above me in the zenith

I didn't know whether the white town
Was coming down from the clouds into me
Or was growing from my womb into the sky

I came back from the journey
To share out the ripened stones from my bundle
Here on the city square

THE UPPER FORTRESS

You open wide your arms you the Tall
Before all the gates of the white town

You welcome the seer sources
The blind sun-shrines the wailing rivers
And the widow mountains

You feed them out of your hand
With dew gathered each morning
From your verses

You join together the surviving syllables
Metals plants and beasts
Into the first word of love

And you build
The last impregnable rampart
Of your fortress in the air

TERAZIJE

To some you are a city square
On the breast of the white town

The left and right suns
Weigh out on you
Their light and darkness

The dealers in clouds
In souls and yawns
Set out their wares on you

Fire-eaters and lightning-walkers
And thunder-tamers
Show off their skills on you

To us you are a stone hand
We read a life-line on you

We have never seen its end

APOTHECARIES' FIELD

I met you old man shepherd
In the white town

You were passing a little after midnight
Through the burning field of Apothecaries
Between the shadows of houses and limetrees

You were carrying a live wolfling on your shoulders
Playing on a lime leaf

Two sparks were dancing over your sheepskin
Kissing your red beard and your hands

I didn't try to stop you
I'd have hit my head on an old limetree

I didn't want to get involved
In apothecaries' business
Their fire here has a guilty conscience

I picked a leaf from a limetree
And took up your melody

FEARLESS TOWER

All day you look at your naked reflection
In the river of paradise

You turn around
And reveal to the white town
Your eight stone thighs

All night you fly through the sky
And fight black fires
For the sun's inheritance

At dawn you're shining on the bank again

Flocks of torch-bearer doves
Remove the traces of blood
From your eight faces

You fear no one
But your father the thunderer

GREAT LORD DANUBE

O great Lord Danube
In your veins flows
The blood of the white town

If you love it get up a moment
From your bed of love

Ride on your biggest carp
Pierce the leaden clouds
And visit your heavenly birthplace

Bring a gift to the white town
Fruits and birds and flowers of paradise

Bring too the stone which can be eaten
And a little air
Of which men do not die

The bell-towers will bow down to you
And the streets prostrate themselves before you
O great Lord Danube

BELGRADE

White bone among the clouds

You arise out of your pyre
Out of your ploughed-up barrows
Out of your scattered ashes

You arise out of your disappearance

The sun keeps you
In its golden reliquary
High above the yapping of centuries

And bears you to the marriage
Of the fourth river of Paradise
With the thirty-sixth river of Earth

White bone among the clouds
Bone of our bones

[1965–1971]

WOLF SALT

THE WORSHIPPING OF THE LAME WOLF
THE FIERY SHE-WOLF
PRAYER TO THE WOLF SHEPHERD
THE WOLF LAND
HYMN TO THE WOLF SHEPHERD
THE LAME WOLF'S TRACKS
THE WOLF BASTARD

The Worshipping of the Lame Wolf

1

Go back to your lair
Lame wolf disgraced

And sleep there
Until the barking freezes
And the curses rust and the torches
Of the hue and cry drop dead

And until they all collapse
Empty-handed into themselves
And bite through their tongues with spite

The dog-headed bullies with knives behind their ears
And the beaters with their members over their
    shoulders
And the hunting dragons the wolf-eaters

On all fours I crawl before you
And howl to your glory
As in your great
Green times

And pray to you my old lame god
Go back to your lair

2

I have prostrated myself before you
Lame wolf

I lie among your images
That are ravaged and burning
And masked in mud

I have fallen among them
My face in your sacred nettles
And burn with them together

My mouth is full
Of their wooden flesh
And golden eyebrows

I have prostrated myself before you
Growl as a sign for me to rise
Lame wolf

3

Accept my poor gifts
Lame wolf

I bring on my shoulders an iron sheep
And a drop of mead in my mouth
To keep your jaws busy

And a little living water in my hand
For you to practise miracles

And a garland of irises
Woven to fit your head
To remind you who you are

And a sample of the very latest wolf-traps
For you to study well

Accept my gifts
Don't scatter them with your godly tail
Lame wolf

4

Turn your face on me
Lame wolf

And inspire me with fire from your jaws
That in your name I may sing
In our ancestral limetree tongue

Inscribe on my brow with your claw
The heavenly signs and runes
That I may grow to be the interpreter of your silence

And bite my left hand
That your wolves may bow to me
And acclaim me their shepherd

Turn your face on me
Stop staring at your toppled image
Lame wolf

5

Lift the stone from your heart
Lame wolf

And show me how you transform
The stone into a sun-bearing cloud
And the cloud into a deer with gold antlers

And if it doesn't weary you show me
How you transform the deer into a white basil flower
And the basil into a six-winged swallow

And show me if you still remember
How you transform the swallow into a fire-serpent
And the serpent into a precious stone

Lift the stone from your heart
And lay it on mine
Lame wolf

6

Let me approach you
Lame wolf

Let me pluck
Three wonder-working hairs
From your three-cornered head

Let me touch with my staff
The star on your brow the stone on your heart
And your left and right ears

And let me kiss
Your wounded godly paw
Cushioned on a cloud

Let me approach you
Don't frighten me with a sacred yawn
Lame wolf

7

Go back to your lair
Lame wolf

And sleep there
Until your coat changes
And you cut your new iron teeth

Sleep until the bones of my ancestors
Blossom and branch out
And break through the earth's crust

Sleep until your lair quakes
And falls in on you

Sleep until your tribe
From the other side of heaven
Wakes you with baying

Go back to your lair
I will visit and tend you in your sleep
Lame wolf

The Fiery She-Wolf

1

The she-wolf lies
In heaven's foothills

Her body a live coal
Is overgrown with grass
And covered with sun-pollen

The mountains in her breast
Rise menacing
And fall forgiving

Through her veins rivers howl
In her eyes lakes flash

In her measureless heart
Metallic ores melt from love
On the sevenfold fire

Wolves play over her back
And live in her crystal womb
To their first and from their final howl

2

They imprison the she-wolf
In subterranean fire

There they force her to build
Towers of smoke
And to make bread of embers

They force-feed her with burning coals
And as drink
Give boiling quicksilver milk

They drive her to couple
With red-hot pokers
And rusty gimlets

With her teeth the she-wolf catches
A fair-haired star
And pulls herself back to heaven's foothills

3

They catch the she-wolf in steel traps
Stretched from horizon to horizon

They take the golden mask from her snout
And tear the secret grass
From between her haunches

They bind her and set on her
Tracker and wind-borer dogs
To defile her

They hack her to pieces
And leave her
To the vultures' talons

With the stump of her tongue the she-wolf catches
Living water from the clouds' jaws
And puts herself together again

4

The she-wolf bathes in the blue
And washes the dog-ash off her body

Deep in the torrents
Flowing down her motionless face
Lightning spawns

In her gaping jaws
The moon hides its axe by day
The sun its knives by night

The beating of her copper heart
Stills the yapping distances
And lulls the twittering air

In the chasms
Below the forests of her eyebrows
Thunderbolts are ready for anything

5

The she-wolf rises on her hindlegs
In heaven's foothills

She rises together with the wolves
Turned to stone in her womb

She rises slowly
Between noon and midnight
Between two wolf-pits

She rises painfully
Dragging her snout free from one pit
Her great tail from the other

She rises with a salty howl
Stuck in her dry gullet

She rises dead with thirst
Towards the clear point at the top of heaven
Towards the watering-place of the long-tailed stars

Prayer to the Wolf Shepherd

1

We pray to you wolf shepherd

Put us round your neck
So we needn't ride day and night
On ourselves

Feed us from your hand
So we needn't eat raw earth
And drink our own blood

Make a little room for us on your shoulders
So we needn't sleep far from ourselves
In the echoes of our howling

Find the newborn red stone
Fled from our breasts
So we needn't chase it to the world's end

We pray to you wolf shepherd

2

Beat us to death or accept us
As we are tattered maimed
And headless

We pray to you wolf shepherd

Clothe us in the hides
Stretched over the beaters' drums

Arm us with the paws
Made into handles
Of hunters' knives

Plant in our jaws the teeth
Strung in necklaces
Of bedworthy bitches

Adorn our necks with the heads
Nailed up on the walls
Of all-knowing watch-towers

We pray to you wolf shepherd

3

Seize our father unfather
With his heart of lead
With his great head of ossified ages

We pray to you wolf shepherd

Get him up from his sleeping-place
So he stops begetting and impaling us
With the sickle that hangs between his legs

Catch him in the act
Here in the middle of Nowhereland
Today on the day of St Never

Deliver him into our paws

So we can give him a taste of his sickle
And tear apart his great body
Of raw time

We pray to you wolf shepherd

4

Break your staff in three
Make it a three-winged eagle
And take us up from here

We pray to you wolf shepherd

Take us up into the felled grove
Of our young ancestors
The moon's daughter and the sun's son

Take us up into the constellation
Of the Great Wolf

We pray to you wolf shepherd

Take us up into our mother's
Crystal womb
Crammed with dog-seed

Take us up from here
At least to the crossroads in the air
That our baying has reached

We pray to you wolf shepherd

5

Don't leave us here alone
To chase up and down
Over our lolling tongue

We pray to you wolf shepherd

Visit us too in our dreams
As you do the old silver wolf
So we can devour you

We pray to you wolf shepherd

Fill our bellies
With your eloquent flesh
Tasting of the great grey cloud

We pray to you wolf shepherd

Dissolve in our blood
Your fragrant wisdom
All made of the salt of salts

We pray to you wolf shepherd

The Wolf Land

1

Father I cannot see our sunny land
The wolf is wreathing her up to the sky
With his black howling

He seems to be pulling her up
By her very roots
Together with her golden heart
And his own bruised one

He senses an untimely death
His own or hers
Or the death of the three-headed sun above her

Does he fear for himself father
Or for her the sunny one

2

My son I see our land asleep
The wolf is licking her cheeks

With his fiery tongue he enlightens her
And she smiles in her sleep
As if burning at the stake

He casts his grey shadow over her
And she ages in her sleep
As if drowning beneath the ash

Is he preparing my son
To swallow her as she sleeps
Or only making sure
She is alive not dead

3

Father I cannot see our beautiful land
The wolf is kneeling on her

With one paw he is caressing
Or slowly strangling her
With the other he claws to blood
The louring sky above him

The hair on his back has the shine
Of a love herb
Or a hate herb
As on the day of his birth

Is the wolf slavering father
Over her bitter flesh
Or is he only worshipping her beauty

4

My son I see our land crucified
Between four grindstones
On which the wolf is sharpening his teeth

The wolf is bending over her
And is reflected angry
In her green eyes

Sparks from the grindstones
Form halo after halo
Around his beautiful head

The four grindstones could say my son
Whether the wolf is sharpening his teeth
For her the crucified
Or for those who crucified her

5

Father I see the wolf
With the young moon's horns on his head
On his horns he is carrying
Our virginal land

He carries her and she does not resist
As if she were dead
Or like to die of love

He carries her along no earthly path

He is carrying her somewhere in the heights
Perhaps to his lair in the sky
Which he plans to dig
For her and for himself

Is he stealing her from us father
Or on the contrary rescuing her

6

Through the wolf's ribs my son
I see our promised land
She has the form of the Easter lamb

The wolf's heart gives her light
In the crimson sea

Either she was swallowed long ago
And now is neither alive nor dead
Or she is just ready
For a second birth

It depends on the wolf's hunger
And on our guiding star
Not on anything else my son

Hymn to the Wolf Shepherd

1

Rejoice O wolf shepherd

From our male pelvis
Fertile by the lean earth
A maiden limetree has grown

From the root
A spring of crimson milk
Flows towards you

In the trunk
A swarm of bees is making
Paternal honey for you

In the crown
Embracing each other
Raven peacock and eagle sing to you

Rejoice O wolf shepherd

2

We've wrenched ourselves out of our paws
Pulled ourselves out of our teeth
Got out of our skins

Rejoice O wolf shepherd

Of our backbone
We've formed a hoop around the world
Criss-crossed our other bones

We've found the axle hole
In which when we were alive
The runaway red stone revolved

Your good teachings
Are now in full flower
Flaming in the weeds above us

Rejoice O wolf shepherd

3

Around us white-fleeced she-clouds
Are peacefully lambing
And thunderbolts are making love
To our beautiful memories

Rejoice O wolf shepherd

Muzzles are rusting in the rain
And gnawing the sandy mounds
That look like our great bodies

Gap-toothed wolf-traps are catching
At stray howls of wind
And snapping the empty air

With our jaws now independent
We chew the white dog-stone
And transform it into nourishing silver

Rejoice O wolf shepherd

4

We fly to meet you
On your unearthed staff

Rejoice O wolf shepherd

We've strung our vertebrae on the staff
Stuck our ribs into its patterns
Thrust our skull on top

Rejoice O wolf shepherd

We've overcome the whirlwinds the beaters
Flown across the pits and stakes
And the snares in the air

Rejoice O wolf shepherd

We fly to meet you
To look into your eyes
And express our joy

Rejoice O wolf shepherd

5

Rejoice O red shadow
Overarching our joy

Rejoice O only tooth mark
On the round world's belly

Rejoice O thunderous word
In the jaws of no-time

Rejoice O black howling
Above the endless snowy oblivion

Rejoice O lighted smile
In the heart of the dog-darkness

Rejoice O golden remembering
Growing over our bones

Rejoice O wolf shepherd

The Lame Wolf's Tracks

1

On their shoulders the beaters carry
The huge lame wolf

From between his bared fangs
His severed male sign swings
Drags in the dust
And leaves an unreadable track

In one of his ears is stuck
A bunch of stubble
In the other a bouquet of burdock

From his slit belly pokes out
Defiled sacred straw

The beaters and assembled dogs
And the flies on his wounds
And the pole of shame
All believe he is dead

2

With his paws the lame wolf strokes the axe
Driven into the hairy cloud

He kisses her slender body
Of fragrant oak
And her two silver cheeks
And her invincible blade

And cleaves himself
Into two living halves

One half comes to rest below earth
The other flies up to heaven

Somewhere in the middle
Between earth and heaven
His vast incandescent heart is left

A new red star is shining
Waiting for its inhabitants

3

On a burning *gusle*
The lame wolf flies below earth

He whips its belly with the bow
And fondles
Its string in flame

With his teeth he scrapes from its neck
The marks of dog bites

He gnaws its wooden horse-head
And with the maplewood pap he dresses
The wound on his right front paw

He spurs it on with his three good paws
Heads it towards the howling
That comes from the heart of earth

Under him the *gusle* whimpers
Spits out fire
And swallows up the darkness

4

On his back the lame wolf carries
A great black eagle
And flies with her through the sky

He drinks dew from her beak
And eats sides of white-fleeced mists

In his jaws he gathers for her
Living star eggs
Buried deep in the blue

He defends her from flying dogs
And predator shears

He strikes her with his tail
And shows her the secret path
From one lair in the sky to another

The eagle pecks his head
Thrusts her talons into his ribs
And stops him falling asleep

5

The lame wolf walks the world
One paw treads the sky
The others earth

He walks backwards
Wiping out each track in front of him

He walks half-blind
With terrible bloodshot eyes
Full of dead stars and living bugs

He walks with a millstone
Jammed round his neck
An old tin can
Tied to his tail

He walks without resting
Out of one ring of dog-heads
Into another

He walks with the twelve-faced sun
On his tongue which lolls to the ground

The Wolf Bastard

1

You bark

That I should cover myself with my ears
Tuck my tail between my legs
And clear out of here

You bark

That I should fall on my knees before you
Beat my head on the ground
And crawl off on all fours
Back to where I was born

You bark bark

That I should crawl backwards
And lick up all my father's tracks
Which showed me the way here

You bark bark bark

That I should stuff my fist in my mouth
Bite off my tongue
And stick it in my belt

2

Without asking your leave
I go on being born as before
From wolf-flowers

I am suckled by the shade of the old she-wolf
That you beat to death with stone testicles
Her and her cubs together

I talk to myself
On the profaned field of fire
Which overarches the confluence
Of memory and foresight

I sing without ceasing

For fear I might be left alone
Among you until death
And after

3

I go on a search for my true father
Who cannot be born without me

I search for him

In the lines of his face
Scattered over the lair
I have fallen into

In the valley bitten out of my foot
Inherited from him
Poor sun-stealer

In the tall weeds
Sprung up between the syllables
Of his name

I search for him
And so my whole life passes
Here on this field of fire

4

With hammer fist and head
I beat on the anvil all day
Invisibly chained to it

My anvil is drenched with dew
Black in the morning green at noon
Red in the evening

I forge old iron
And scraps of moonlight

I burn with desire
To discover the metal
My chain is forged from

A great grey cloud
Sits on my right shoulder
And guides my hand

Young wolves
Hidden by day in my lair
Watch me are silent and learn

5

From the brotherly constellation of Seven Sheepboys
I drive my wolves down
Into the main square of your city

Together with them we glare at you
And easily drive you
Into your multistoreyed kennels

I revel in the blind internecine battle
Of your domestic iron monsters
Crazed without you

I climb on my wolves' backs
And with my teeth pull the crossed knives
Down from your highest towers

And bay the moon to my heart's content
With my long-tailed sons

6

Astride my head-wolf
I return to the green heights
That I left to come down here

There I dig myself a grave
In the wolf shepherd's deepest thought

In that forgotten depth
None of you would dream of looking
For my dead body

There in peace matures
The grey schist called antimony
That I am made of

From it sprouts first
A new wolf-flower
And then all the rest in order

In its sacred green order

7

You bark

That my reason has dropped to my rump
And grown overnight
Into a tail of ill-omen

You bark

That my thoughts have changed
Into grey bristles
And pierced all the pores on my skin

You bark bark

That my words smell
Of human flesh burnt at the stake
And of the white seed of my long-tailed god

You bark bark bark

That out of my throat comes
A familiar bloodthirsty howl
Which I call a song

Just you bark

[1972–1975]

RAW FLESH

EARTHLY CONSTELLATION

In the light from the shop
On Gudurica Street in Vršac
Three old workmen are drinking
Their evening beer from bottles

The metal tops have formed
A constellation on the strip of earth
Between pavement and road

It glimmers in the dusk
And waits for its own star-gazer

I'd come just to get cigarettes
I ask for a bottle of beer
To find my star its place too

THE IDOL OF VRŠAC

I hold him on my hand

He used to hold the sun
In his wolf teeth

Godly he played with it
Carried it up to heaven
Carried it down below earth

He's formed of the clay
Of which as a child by the River Karaš
I made little men
And solemnly ate them

He won't tell me anything
About himself about the earth he sees again

Even though I'm an old Vrščanin

REJUVENATED WATERFALL

We three living and two shades
Wanted to revisit
The secret place of our youth

Our waterfall
Somewhere on Vršac Hill
I can't say where

We're standing by the waterfall
It's close we can hear it
But we can't see it

It's overgrown with young brushwood
And yellow thorn flowers

One of us mutters between his teeth

Lucky thing
It can dissolve and crystallize
Its years in itself

THE UNKNOWN CITIZEN

The astroragler Winey Grapeson was born
Once and for all in Vršac

He was washed in wine
And swaddled in vine leaves

His first toy was
A telescope for reading heavenly letters
Botched together from maize stalks

He lived among people by day
By night among stars

When his time came to die
He moved into the body
Of some second-sighted fellow citizen

Any of us Vrščani
Might be him in person
But won't own up to it

Me too I shrug my shoulders

IN THE VILLAGE OF MY FOREFATHERS

One hugs me
One looks at me with wolf eyes
One takes off his hat
So I can see him better

Each one asks me
Do you know who I am

Unknown old men and women
Usurp the names
Of boys and girls of my memory

And I ask one of them
Tell me old chap
Is George Kurja
Still alive

That's me he answers
In a voice from the other world

I stroke his cheek with my hand
And silently beg him to tell me
Whether I am alive still too

THE LOST RED BOOT

My great-grandmother Sultana Urošević
Used to sail the sky in a wooden trough
And catch rain-bearing clouds

With wolf-balms and others
She did many more
Great and small miracles

After her death
She went on meddling
In the business of the living

They dug her up
To teach her to behave
And to bury her better

She lay there rosy-cheeked
In her oaken coffin

On one foot she was wearing
A little red boot
With splashes of fresh mud

To the end of my life I'll search
For that other boot she lost

TIME SWEPT UP

The sweeper collects dry leaves with his broom
Under the chestnut trees
Along the Avenue

He stops under each tree
And shakes it with all his might

He'd like autumn to hurry up

If he had his way
Vršac would be left in a flash
Without autumn and the other seasons

He'd be left
With his broom to gnaw

I'd warn him
Only a chestnut
Got stuck in my throat

THE LAST DANCE

I am burying my mother
In the old overcrowded
New Cemetery of Belgrade

The coffin is laboriously lowered
Into the shallow slit of grave
And rests on my father's

It soon disappears under the first clods

Two hatless young grave-diggers
Leap round on the invisible coffin
And pack down the earth

On their upraised spades
Shine two afternoon suns

My laughing mother
Would have been thrilled to watch
This dance in her honour

WALKING IN A CIRCLE

for the shade of Gary Firneiss

Long past midnight
I'm walking with a childhood friend
Round the Graben in Vienna

After so many years apart
We find we are revealing
The same things to each other

We talk about
The shape of freedom

We talk about the circle
Which is closing
Which must close

To be freed
From its beginning and its end

After that how can I say
It was
Our last walk

UNBROKEN LESSON

The red teacher Žarko Zrenjanin
Was killed by the crook-limbed master-men

Our ordinary men swear
They still see him

On the derailed train full of murderers
In the burning cornfield
In the centre of Vršac ringed by dogs

Only we his pupils
Know what's going on

Ignoring the master-laws
We're giving him our hearts' work
And our weapons

THE POET'S LADDER

In Vršac on the eve of war
Dejan Brankov the poet took a flat
In the house next to ours

He asked me to persuade my father
To set up a ladder
On our side of the wall

Any night he expected
They'd come to take him
To the concentration camp

Long after he'd been killed
Leading a band of partisans
The ladder still stood
In its appointed place

Up the wooden rungs there climbed
A muscat vine

IMMINENT RETURN

In a cell of Bečkerek Prison
I spend the day with a Red Army man
Who'd escaped from a prison camp

Any moment the door may open
And he'll be taken out
And shot in the yard

He asks me to show him
The quickest way
To Moscow

With breadcrumbs on the floor
I build the towns he'd pass

He measures the distance with his finger
Claps me on the shoulder with his great hand
And rocks the whole prison with his shout

You're not far my beauty

BE SEEING YOU

After the third evening round
In the yard of the concentration camp
We disperse to our quarters

We know that before dawn
One of us will be taken out and shot

We smile like conspirators
And whisper to each other
Be seeing you

We don't say when or where

We've given up the old ways
We know what we mean

POETRY LESSON

We're sitting on the white bench
Under the bust of Lenau

We're kissing
And just incidentally talking
About poetry

We're talking about poetry
And just incidentally kissing

The poet is looking out through us
Through the white bench
Through the gravel on the path

And is so splendidly silent
With his splendid bronze lips

In Vršac Park
I'm slowly learning
What really matters in a poem

AT THE SIGN OF THE WOLVES

Within reach of the last houses of town
On the highroad they found the horses killed
Harnessed to an empty cart

And in the mulberry tree by the road
The merchant changed into a white sheep

All night the wolves danced round the tree
Which smelt of human flesh

You'd soon have struck a bargain
With the long-tailed dancers
Grandma tells me

I stare at her wolf teeth
And try to guess her laughter

I run into the back garden
Climb the snow-laden pear tree
And practise wolf-howls

NOT QUITE NICE

A coffin is passing down the street

They send me to wake grandpa
Nikola Urošević Suču

So-and-so has died I tell him

Grandpa opens one eye
And grunts always the same thing

What's come over him
He's never done anything
Like that before

He turns over
And snoozes off again

THE GAME OF CREATION

We kids from kindergarten
Play during break
In the church close in Vršac

We choose one to be the hill
Another to be the river

The hill makes two steps
By holding out his hands

The river pulls out his willy
And sends a thin trickle
From one hand over the other to the ground

The rest of us yell
Wa-ter-spout
Out Out Out

And beg to be given
The chief rôles in the game

WOLF ANCESTRY

Under the limetrees in Sand
My great-grandfather Ilija Luka Morun
Found two wolflings

He put them between his donkey's ears
And brought them to the fold

He fed them on sheep's milk
And taught them to play
With the lambs of their own age

When they were strong he took them back
To the same place under the limetrees
Kissed them and signed them with the cross

Ever since childhood I've been waiting
For my years to equal
Great-grandfather's

To ask him
Which of those wolflings
Was me

WOLF EYES

Before my christening I was given
The name of one of the brothers
That the she-wolf suckled

All her life grandma will call me
In her flaxen Vlach tongue
Wolfling

Secretly she used to give me
Raw meat to eat
So I'd grow to be head-wolf

I believed
My eyes would begin to shine
In the dark

My eyes don't shine yet
Probably because the real dark
Hasn't yet begun to fall

THE WOLVES' FOSTER-FATHER

On a sleigh laden
With salt and smugglers
My great-grandfather Ilija Luka Morun
Flies through Sand

Wolves howl and attack
Both horses and men

Great-grandfather threatens
He'll kill on the spot
Anyone who draws a gun

He stands up and howls more fiercely
Than the long-tailed brigands

The wolves howl mournfully
And gradually drop behind the horses
Who have somehow got wings

As fewer winters and fewer snows
Separate me from great-grandfather
I hear his wolf-voice more clearly

THE WHITE BOAT

A white boat's run aground
On the very top of the Hill

None of the men of Vršac knows
Where she came from through the sky
Nor where she was heading

She's stowed the Tower in her belly
Together with the frozen sun
And is waiting for a fair wind

We children clear the snow from the path
And with our wooden shovels send her
Contradictory signals

BROKEN HORNS

My grandfather Miloš Popa Nemac
In all his life spoke fewer words
Than a man born dumb they say

But he could get his shoulders
Under a green ox
And slowly lift it off the ground

The ox would paw the air
With all four feet
And toss his horns at the sky

People stood round in a circle
Threw up their fur caps
And crossed themselves backwards

In my dreams I beg grandfather
To tell me where to find
Our ancient god of the herds

Grandfather stands before me dumb
With broken horns on his head

THE NEXT WORLD

On little boards grandma sets
Cakes with lighted candles

She whispers messages over them
To the dead men and women of our blood
And lets them float down the Karaš

The boards slide over the black water
The candles penetrate the dusk
And disappear round the bend in the river

Grandma declares
They've arrived safely
In the next world

I've been in that world already
And set bird-traps there

Only I didn't know
That in the flowering willows I was snaring
My own kinsmen

WOLVES' TENDERNESS

We're lying in the grass
On Wolf-Meadow above Vršac

They say
The wolves were killed here
Every last one

Only their name
Was left alive

An animal tenderness reaches us
From under the alert grass

And stirs our lips
And limbs and blood

We love each other without a word
My young she-wolf and I

THE CHERRY TREE IN THE HOUSE OF DEATH

for Ion Marcoviceanu

Little Jovica Agbaba got hold of
A handful of cherries
And smuggled them into the camp

He counted them out and divided them
Into three equal parts

We ask him where he puts the stones

He swallows them
So as to fill himself more quickly

We stare at the red fruit
On the branches of the cherry tree
Growing out of his belly

And all three suddenly
Burst out laughing

ABSOLUTE GOAL

Two Red Army men are carrying
Their dead comrade past our house

A little while ago my mother was feeding
All three with apple tart
And Vršac wine

My father advised the dead man
They should go over the roofs
And come out behind the nest of machine-guns

The dead man laughed hugged my father
And together with the other two
Chose a short cut

I watch the Red Army men

They put their comrade in a cart
Painted with the crooked letters
T o   B e r l i n

MAN'S JOB

Before dawn they wake us
And line us up
In the concentration camp

In the roll-call of death
The gypsy's name rings out

The gypsy tucks his fiddle under his arm
And leaves
The line of the living

The roll-caller jeers
He won't need his instrument

The gypsy draws himself up

Do you suppose
Death will find me
Some better job

CONVERSATION WITH POPPIES

Near Vršac coming home
I turn off the road into the young corn
Among the poppies

Neca Ankucić knotted
A borrowed red scarf round her head
And went singing to the scaffold

She was a real poppy
Those who saw her told me

I ask after
Her green years
That never sprouted

ENDLESS YOUTH

My childhood friend Gary Firneiss
Has died

Through the streets of Vienna
I run away from myself

I don't know where to look
At houses at cars at people
I can't

Behind each I see
A shadow
Biding its time

I look at the sky

Death stands blue above me
Becoming one
With a sort of endless youth

HOW LIKE THE FAMILY

You've become a proper wolf
I haven't seen you for ages
But I knew you at once
A relation from Vršac tells me

I roar with laughter

Instead of explaining nicely
That what he sees before him
Is the ponderous sleepy beast
That has devoured me

SECRET JOKE

With the dusk
The Vršac grave-diggers invade
The inn on the Jabuka road

They're bellowing with laughter
And shout from the door their order
Two yards of wine

The innkeeper brings full glasses
And arranges them crosswise on the table
A yard wide and a yard long

Together with the grave-diggers
My eyes drink up
Their secret joke

WOLF SHADOW

They say my great-grandmother
The witch Sultana Urošević
Had a she-wolf's shadow

By moonlight she never
Went out of doors

So no one should tread on her shadow
Take her secret powers
And kill her on the spot

They say
It's from great-grandmother I have
These eyes and this tongue

I don't know about the wolf shadow

By moonlight always
And often by sunlight
I walk backwards

Just in case

MEETING WITH MY FOREFATHERS

I climb up to the family chapel
In Grebenac cemetery

The wooden doors are closed
But don't prevent me
Seeing my forefathers

They ride garlanded rams
Over this dry sea-bed
Called Banat

They get on better with wolves
Than with people
And bow only to the sun
Each morning and evening

They wear hemp shirts
Smeared with tallow
And walk with the step of highborn lords

I go to meet them
To hear who and what they are

PROTECTOR OF THE CORN

I meet a fine old man
On the Vršac-Belgrade train

He's going to the third stop
Just so that on the way
He can see the corn

He looks through the open window
Nods his head now and then

And all the time he's flying
Clothed in golden spikes of wheat
Above the ripe fields

He'll go back to Vršac by the first train

With a handful of grain in his pocket
With two ears of corn stuck in his hat

HEAVENLY JOURNEY

On the photo
Taken on a hill above Jabuka
You can see my earthly companion and me

We're holding hands
She's in a summer dress cut square
I'm in a shirt with the sleeves rolled up

We've stepped off the top of the hill
On to the level sky before us

On the photo
Taken thirty years ago
You can't see which star we've reached

The camera caught us from behind
You won't read anything
From our faces

THE CHARIOT OF VRŠAC

Our ancient god of earth and of forgetting
Has reared upright between two wheels

He's chewing over the last grains
Of his wolf-silence
And patience

Like this without the sun his toy
He is no one and nothing

His sacred paws are waiting
Tense and ready

I beg him to remember
At least us men of Vršac
When he flies up again

BEAUTIFUL NOTHINGNESS

If Sterija walks as he did in life
Down the Jabuka road every evening
I might easily meet him

I'd remind him
That in one place he wrote
Vršac is a beautiful town

In another
All is nothingness

With a little skill
From these two statements
I might draw the conclusion

Nothingness is beautiful

With a little good will
He great poet and great wit
Might agree

[1972–1973]

THE HOUSE IN THE HIGHROAD

I DEFEND

They would bury my gaze
In the dust
Rip the rose of my smile
From my lips

I guard the first
Spring in my breast
I guard the first
Tear of joy

They would divorce me
From freedom
They would plough up
My soul my soul

I defend
This bit of heaven in my eyes
I defend
This bit of earth in my hand

They would cut down
My young orchard of joy
Yoke my songs' nightingales
To a wooden plough

I won't give up
This bit of sun in my eyes
I won't give up
This bit of bread in my hand

1950

LETTER TO A FRIEND FROM ABROAD

They offered you
The eyes of their newspapers
They offered you
The gilt heart of a marionette

Here you saw a rainbow
Above the storm in our breasts
Back home you stayed faithful
To your heart

They built a pale wall round you
A wall of silence
They built a dark wall round you
A wall of lies

You didn't hush up
The hard-won songs of your hands
You didn't forget
The sharp air of freedom

You didn't lie to the future
Whose hand you had clasped

1950

STEĆAK

In the pathlessness
An upraised hand
Flamed with its palm
Flashed with its fingers

Long ago it freed
The old native sun
Tied to the tails
Of foreign stallions

Today it illuminates
The cavern of riddles
Hollowed out by questions
In my brow of stone

An upraised hand
Wordless met me
In the pathlessness
And showed me the way

1952

PEACE-BEARING SONG

The warriors clean their weapons
And boast of the battle
They won tomorrow
They'll win yesterday

The singers give the song sacramental wine
From the cloud of glory

The song struggles sober
Complains to itself

In the song the singers are precious stones
The warriors a fiery serpent
Which gives birth to the stones and eats them

In the song the song is wind
The last wind the fire-bearer

The warriors fly with the singers
On the drunken cloud of glory
And sing a song they cannot hear

1963

BELGRADE LIBRARY

Bibliophobic fires
Set light to her
To gut our memories

We raised her again
Above the prophetic ashes

Entry is free to all

Who wish to learn
To read from stars
And people's hearts

Her doors are barred
To fiery revenants
Who refuse to learn their letters

1973

NOVI SAD: NEW ORCHARD IN BLOSSOM

It has grown from the palms of workers
Who lord it today
Over the Dukeries of the plain

It spreads branches of brick
Sun-mortar and moon-glass

It has bridged the ancient river
And recognizes its youthful heights
In a liquid mirror

It has climbed the starry mountain belfry
To hear its name pronounced
In consonant tongues

It blossoms heedless
Of the season

1980

The Wall

1

Eye to eye with the wall

I'm not fair or foul
I've no face

Breast to breast with the wall

I'm not strong or weak
I've no experience

Face to face with the wall

I'm not good or bad
I'm alone

2

If I were lichen
Its darkness too would burst

If I were fungus
Its peace too would squeal

If I were lightning
Its shadow too would fall on its knees

3

Burn out grass

Why do you shine bright
On this drubbing-stone

Here I've no steps

Go back heaven
To your place

Why do you show blue
Between the plaster clouds

Here I've no eyes

4

And you
With hair of rain and adam's apples of wind
Go back you too

Why do you appear to me
In the flight of whitewash butterflies

Here I've no heart

In front of the wall
I too become wall

[1952]

Armed Goodness

to the Spanish guerillas

1

The sky the sky is blue
The Guadalquivir flows on

The impossible continues

2

In despair
There's no pole star
We'll have to set light to our hearts

There are no comforting vistas
We'll have to pack a little vastness
In the bags under our eyes

There's no way out of despair
We'll have to smash down the gates

Smash them with a copper bull
Its horns branching
Into a blazing orange tree

3

Years years
But not a single day

May wrath take flame

Great fruitful words
But not a single olive tree

May the blow give birth

So the ribs of twofold absurdity
Will burst open

So the stake of shame will grow leaves

4

The earth the earth is dumb

Cypresses rise
Rise and fall

The impossible continues

But even armed
Goodness never stops

[1952]

The Eyes of Sutjeska

1

Dog unspeakable dog
One jaw in the cloud
The other in the dust
You've swallowed everything we had

Everything we forged in death
Under your palate
On the fire of our bones

May your hunger swallow you too

We who survived on the naked heart's crag
Without anyone anywhere anything anywhere
Must create everything anew

Create earth anew
Heaven anew

May your jaws rot dog

2

Sutjeska rises up to the cloud
Grapples with the sun-eater

Sutjeska blind turns round herself
Can't find her own banks

3

Here all lights perish
All meanings hush all paths stop
From here there's nowhere

We've lit great fires
On the crossings of our veins

Here there's no ground under our feet
No vault over our heads
Where to from here

We've all set out with one infinite step
A single step
Through the ravines of our own heads
Set out up the precipice of our dream

4

Sutjeska began to flow towards her source
Towards the sun towards the eye of earth
And met nothing anywhere

Sutjeska blind turned to follow us
She can't think where to flow to next

5

From our raw flesh the earth is born
Clod by clod stone by stone
Certainty by certainty

From our mad breath heaven is born
Serenity by serenity star by star
Horizon by horizon

Our strength grows into mountains into constellations
Our hunger into orchards our tenderness into flowers
Our freedom into endless vistas

More and more we become everything
Nothing can take anything from us

6

Sutjeska thunders through our bones
Flows between the red flowers
In our hearts is her end
In our hearts is her source

Sutjeska turns into a sunbird
With the black dog in her beak

The House in the Highroad

1

Our house stands in the middle of the highroad
Linking the first sun to the last

Our very own gold-handed black fortune
Was the architect

It seems she'd planned a sky-bridge
A pair of sun-scales it seems
But it ended up as a house

2

Since then monsters have streamed out onto the
    highroad
And danger-mongers and thunder-makers
And sun-merchants

Then our beautiful house disappears
In the struggle of earth and sky
In the gnashing of darkness in the screaming of light
In the pounding of hooves on the roof

3

Sky splits from earth now and then

Our house appears in the middle of the highroad
Appears in all its beauty once again

Just like a sky-bridge
Like a pair of sun-scales

4

The highroad goes on minding its own business
Keeps linking the first sun to the last

Only the winds
Employed about the house
Scatter the smell of burning horns

[1956]

BLACK MIGRATIONS

They've thrown their naked days
Out of the house

Into the unquiet up in the rafters
With no windows no doors
There they'll set up home

Their living footprints
Scattered through the rooms
Sob over the wounded air

Frantic roads
Roll their bloody tree trunks

Beneath the hearths beneath the mangers
In the mournful bosom of the fields
Their roots will rot

Above the roofs above the yards
On the forehead of their native sky
Eternal clouds will threaten
A bronze curse

Their pale terrors
With hair ablaze
Hug the empty thresholds

1951

THE POET'S MONUMENT RESURRECTED

Today the demolishers devour
An innocent poet of bronze

The pigeons from the poet's shoulders
Hide beneath the wing of earth

The bloated demolishers have no notion
Of what his verses are building above them

The pigeons will be coming back tomorrow
To light the poet a quill

The demolishers are clutching their heads
Their eyes will drop out of their heads

The pigeons are standing in the air
On top of the invisible monument

1966

THE RED BRASS BAND

for Adriaan van der Staay and Martin Mooij

They play greasepainted
Dressed up in comic costumes
Of imaginary times

Our unruly children with no memory
No inherited sin
No seal on their tongue

They play the songs of our young grandfathers
And still younger grandmothers
And Aux armes citoyens
Arise ye starvelings

And dance and sing
And don't be afraid any more
They play at the end

Around them fall
Paper bastilles
And newly-forged
Invisible chains break

Rotterdam 1974

THE GOLDEN HORN

Every night
Between midnight and twelve
Three seas meet
To bathe the City
They've given birth to

They rinse off its walls
The layers of plots and spices
And errors of all times

Every dawn the city gleams
In the endless blue of now
Just like the moment it appeared

I blow into the Golden Horn
To thank my friends here
For this sight

Istanbul 1974

WOOING THE ROCKS

for Octavio Paz

From the womb of virgin rocks
The Olmecs took blocks single-handed
To build the rain-god's palaces

They ogled the rocks
Listened to their throbbing veins
And cheek stroked cheek

With volcanic stone tied to rods
They bored holes in the rocks' womb
And filled them with bones

With tongues of damp clay
They trapped the wounded places

They laid fires
Warmed the rocks' thighs
And sprinkled them with cold water

After so many proofs of love
The rocks opened by themselves
And gave birth to blocks of the shape desired

Oaxaca 1975

Notes on The House in the Highroad

NOTE ON THE YOUNG WOODCUTTERS

We taught fire love
So our earth would burn no more

from the memorial on the Black Peak, 1961

NOTE ON THE TERAZIJE GALLOWS, 1941

Tell the earth-thieves
To plant no more orchards of death
Beneath this star of ours
Or the fruit will eat them up

1969

NOTE ON THE TROWEL

Dance trowel
Where our heart stood still

from the Vlasotinac memorial, 1975

NOTE ON THE STONE

If you long for our cheeks
Stroke this stone at noon

from the Vlasotinac memorial, 1975

NOTE ON THE EARTH

If you kiss the earth with your step come
If you trample it return traveller

from the Božurnja memorial, 1966

THE CUT

BREAKFAST IN THE BIG CITY

I'm having breakfast in my flat with a cousin
Wolf from green Sand

He licks the honey from his bare clasp-knife
And reveals to me
The shining alphabet of his teeth

You're whirling round with your heads off here
Your feet in your pockets
Your hands in your purses

These floors have sawn you up

You don't know about lofts
And the sky above you
You've got no cellars
And no earth below you

You're just tree trunks in the air here

CRAZY WAY OUT

They scare me by saying
There's a plank loose in my head

They scare me more by saying
They'll bury me
In a box with the planks loose

They scare me but little do they know
That with my planks unhinged
I'll scare them

The happy madman from our street
Boasts to me

THE HOUSE

Together with the first false sun
We had a visit from Agim
The woodchopper from Priština way

He brought us two red apples
Wrapped in a scarf
And the news that he'd finally got a house

You've a roof over your head at last Agim

I've no roof
The wind took it off

You've a door and windows then

I've no door no windows either
The winter tore them out

You've four walls at least

I've not even all four walls
All I've got is a house like I said
The rest'll be easy

THE POPLAR AND THE PASSER-BY

They're widening the street
Clogged with traffic
They're felling the poplars

The bulldozers take a run-up
And with a single blow
Knock down the trees

One poplar just trembled
Withstood the iron

The bulldozer pulls back
From her noisily
Prepares for the final charge

In the huddle of passers-by
There's an elderly man

He takes his hat off to the poplar
Waves his umbrella at her
And shouts at the top of his voice

Don't give in love

HARMONY OF OPPOSITES

Drenched in sweat
The four-eyed worker laughs
And points his iron rod
At the sliding doors of the foundry

See them
They're wide open
Summer and winter

We prefer
Working in winter

The molten iron has
The whiteness of snow
The snow has the whiteness
Of molten iron

And us foundrymen
Are neither hot nor cold

DECLARATION OF LOVE

We were broken dolls
Of plaster and bandages
Filling the hospital waiting room

One doll confides in us

She's a factory girl who tried
To clean a machine while it was running
And lost her left hand

Her man just doesn't know
How to comfort her

Don't you worry my love
From now on I'll cuddle you
With my three hands

SWALLOW LANGUAGE

A crippled old woman
Teacher of foreign languages
Keeps the window of her room
Open all year round

A swallow has built its nest
In the glass of her lampshade

The old woman listens to the twittering
Forges plans for the future

One day when they carry me
Out of this cage
My companion will go on
With my work

She'll teach much better than me
Old frog that I am

POETRY READING FOR THE GASTARBEITERS

Welcome comrade poet
When can you read us your poems

How about after work

After work
The men are tired
They can't wait to get back to their dorms

How about Saturday

Saturday the men tidy up
Wash and mend
And write letters home

How about Sunday

Sunday the men leave the dorms
The young to visit their girls
The old to the station to wait for trains

So you've no time for poetry

We've no time as you can see
But we'll make some together

Rotterdam, 1971

READING FEAR THROUGH

In fear I open a letter
From a friend abroad
The first in thirty years

In even greater fear I read

It seems as if
Nothing moves here

But even this way
You can stay alive

Only we didn't know that
And we've been dying of fear

LEGEND OF THE BIG CITY

Here old buddy
On this scrap of earth
Survivors of fire and flood took refuge

They settled as best they could
On top of each other
In pigeon-lofts piercing the sky

They peck at concrete
Gulp sooty rain-water
Choke in sweaty steel

And while their feathers fly all over
They wait

Till there
In their distant homeland
The fire dies down and the waters retreat

So they can go back
To houses built to their measure
On the slope of a hill grown green
Close by a river gone calm

Till then old buddy
Let's have another drink

New York, 1970

SECRET POST

The poet Octavio Paz tells me

Little postmen with faces of baked clay
Played a big part
In the revolution of the landless

They too paid their debt to the flag
Of Zapata the barefoot general

I follow them on their way
From one poet's Aztec eyes
To the other

They carry from village to village
Letters full of earth and freedom
And plumed serpents and red jaguars

Till late tonight
As far as here in Cuernavaca

CAPE OF GOOD HOPE

for Breyten Breytenbach

At a fair in South Africa
White racists exhibited
A black couple

They made them climb trees
And howl
Crawl on all fours
And eat grass

I was left with a choice
Adds my poet friend

Either I took off my white skin
And hung it on the nail
Or

DISPUTE ABOUT DEW

Fulcanelli's pupil introduces me
To his athanor oven

Taking me by the arm
He leads me out of the workshop
Into the garden behind the house

He shows me the grass
From which he skims the dew
To prepare the Great Work

He bends over my ear

They yell about water being H_2O
And don't dream that clouds
Are planets too

BOWL OF NOURISHING SNOW

The warriors of the army of the poor
Took off their uniforms
Tied the legs and sleeves
And made sacks

On their backs they carried
Seed for sowing
To the war village of Nanivan

From a thirsty valley
They made a sea of rice
From North they made South

And here tonight over a bowl
Full of nourishing snow
Their memories circle

We lived in caves
In heaven in Nanivan

Yenan, 1980

STREET MONSTER

The waxen old woman is melting with fright
Among the curious passers-by

Some monster
Just missed running her over
On a pedestrian crossing

One passer-by asks her
What sort of a monster was it
Male or female

The old woman flickers
She almost blows out

I didn't manage to get a look
Between the monster's wheels

DREAM EDUCATION

I leap from roof to roof
And with an enormous butterfly net
I hunt technocrats bureaucrats
Gnoseocrats

I put the finest examples
In jars of alcohol
And I write out little labels
With their scientific names

I show them to my pupils in the lesson

Together with the dinosaurs
Gigantosauruses tyrannosauruses
Who step down obediently
From the classroom walls

Even you relish my dream
I can see your left ear smiling

A quiet little bug challenges me
My acquaintance the biology teacher

BUILDING

A retired partisan colonel
Spends all his money
And all his free time
On books

His fellow pensioners
Invite him for a walk for a pint
Tease him and ask
What's the use of all that learning

The ex-bricklayer
Taps his grey head
With his forefinger

I don't want to take this pot
Into the earth empty

THE BEAUTIFUL GOD-HATER

A regular customer in a local bar
Waves his empty sleeve
And thunders into his unkempt beard

We've buried the gods
And now it's the turn of the dummies
Who're playing at gods

The customer is hidden in tobacco clouds
And lit up by his own words

Hewn from an oak trunk
He is as beautiful as a god
Recently dug up in Sand

A CRITIQUE OF POETRY

After the poems have been read
At a poetry evening in a factory
The conversation begins

A red-haired listener
Freckles written all over his face
Raises his hand

Comrade poets

If I were to put all my life
Into verse for you
The paper would go red at once

And burst into flames

POEM IN VIEW

We are going to a big working meeting
And looking forward to talking
With our old comrades

We are nearing the hero town

Through the clear water of its name
Shimmer rows of blossoming fruit trees
Verses sprout in my head

New Orchard red under the bark
Novi Sad grows white from afar

OLD AGE IN LEAF

The old revolutionary commander
Leads the cheerful brigades
Of boys and girls

With them he plants birches
Beeches and pines
In ranks among the red flags

He shades his eyes with his hand

I watch these peace-loving saplings
Storming the bare mountains

And see my dead comrades in the flower of youth
With whom I once
Liberated these very mountains

SELF-MANAGERS

A former partisan of our age
Interlocks the fingers of both hands
And conjures up before us
Anti-tank defences on the road

In the war we were as one
In sharing the surplus of death

In peacetime
Why not be as one again
In producing the surplus of life

By ourselves without accountants

THE MAN'S FOUR WHEELS

The din in our street
Day and night
Is driving my good neighbour mad

With his hands he draws circles
Around his ears
And tells me his dream

From my shoulders and my hips
I've grown wheels

I'm revving in the queue
With the other vehicles
Here at the corner of the street

And waiting for the lights to go green

THE FRUITS OF BATTLE

In the battle the barefoot guns
Gained cloth slippers
To climb up the forbidden mountains
To climb up the sky

Now their step is lighter

The mouths of their barrels are loaded
With buds of white flowers
Of bamboo and rice

Now their shooting is unheard of

They're helping their freedoms
To be freed for the second time

My Chinese comrades told me

Peking, 1980

HIGH SCHOOL OF LOVE

Before a storm in the Luxembourg Gardens
My old friend the philosopher
Returns for a moment
To the distant woods of his youth

On an outing in the Carpathians
A storm overtakes our young company

Lightning burns in our hair
Thunder smashes on our necks
And flings us to the ground
Together with the pine trees

The girls shriek for help
The boys don't behave much better

I'm the youngest and I yell at them

Come off it
It's easy for you to die
You've all fucked already

How can I die

Paris, 1975

UNITED APPLES

for Breyten Breytenbach

In Capetown in South Africa
The prison warder plays with his keys
And leers into the poet's face

Just you listen scum
You don't keep to the rules

For lunch you refuse
To eat an apple
And then for days on end
You draw it and write poems about it

Either you obey in future
Or I'll rip
Your father's apple out of your throat

RESPECT FOR THE AXLE

Those ancient peoples the Incas
Mayas Olmecs Aztecs
Didn't know about the wheel

As if they couldn't see
That the sun doesn't walk across the sky

In a grave however
Archaeologists have found
A children's toy
A cart on wheels

It never occurred to adults
To play with them

Their descendant my host
Draws with his hand
The wheel of the view

Our ancestors didn't believe
That their backbone
Was the axle of the world

Cuernavaca, 1975

RASTKO PETROVIĆ'S GRAVE

An old charwoman from my country
Heard I'd visited
Rastko's grave in Rock Creek
Cemetery in Washington

Every year she says
On feastdays I make cakes
And light candles
For my dead in the old country

And for the Indians of the Osceola tribe
Since my neighbours told me
Their cemetery lies here
Underneath the houses of our block

Now I'll look after
That Serbian poet too

He's got nobody here either

POET'S REFUGE

to the memory of Veronica Porumbacu
Tolya Baconsky Milo Petroveanu
and Mihai Gafiţa

A few poets old friends
Met for supper
In a house in Bucharest

The earthquake broke into their supper
And crashed the house to the ground

The salvage team is looking for them
In the wreckage of concrete glass
Flesh and rags

A young soldier flings out his arms
White with plaster to the elbows

We won't find them here
They're in their poems

THE TALL SILENT ONES

In the far-off forests of Sweden
There are people who don't spend
More than two hundred words

Tells Artur Lundkvist
A seventy-year-old pine

I listen to him

And hear those people
They know all the tongues of trees
And beasts and blizzards

What use have they for mountains
Of their own words

THE BETROTHED OF DEATH

My little old countryman of corn-straw
Dozes lonely all day
Nailed to his easy chair

He doesn't take his eyes off the door
As he turns to me whispering

I wasn't even afraid of life
Never mind of her
I wait for her night by night

I can't howl any more
And call for help

I lie awake in bed
With the kitchen knife on my chest
And my arms crossed over the blade

THE ORIGIN OF LOVE

I'm waiting for the sun on a bench
In the park opposite my house

I follow the path of the clouds across the sky
And of the couples arm in arm
On the gravel between the pines

The newspaper reader at the other end of the bench
Follows the path of my gazes

Love hasn't always existed
The poor invented it you know

To get at women's sweet locks
And men's straight keys
Without silver shillings

HAND-READING

A workers' delegate is sitting beside me
At an interminable meeting

Deafened like me like all of us
By the rustling of papers
And of papery phrases

He goes to the rostrum
Examines the life-lines
On his bare hands
And begins

In the factory at the machine
I think all day too
With my hands

That doesn't mean I leave
My head in the changing room

And so

LIMETREE REVENANTS

The builder from my home-town
Can't forget the felling
Of the avenue of trees in his street

He covers his eyes with his hands

In my dreams I'm attacked by birds
With wings of lime leaves

TROUBLE WITHIN TROUBLE

to the people of the Montenegrin coast
in the earthquake of 1979

The bareheaded fisherman stands on the shore
And with his gaze digs through
The sated mass of water

He complains more to his shadow
Than to the passers-by

Some great misfortune
Forced the sea
To come suddenly into our homes
Through closed doors

We tried our best
To receive her properly
Though we didn't even have
A crumb of time

Our dead can tell you that

ADVICE AND A HALF

Before you die dear neighbour
You need a good sleep

That's the advice of my acquaintance
A tramp in the local park

And he doesn't move from the bench
Where he's lazing

BIG CITY POEM

The other day my wife
For whom I would do anything
Said to me

I wish I had
A little green tree
To run along the street behind me

[1970–1980]

from IRON GARDEN

THE LITTLE BOX

THE LITTLE BOX

The little box grows her first teeth
And her little length grows
Her little width her little emptiness
And everything she has

The little box grows and grows
And now inside her is the cupboard
She was in before

And she grows and grows and grows
And now inside her is the room
And the house and town and land
And the world she was in before

The little box remembers her childhood
And by wishing really hard
Becomes a little box again

Now inside the little box
Is the whole world all teeny-weeny
Easy to slip in your pocket
Easy to steal easy to lose

Look after the little box

THE LITTLE BOX'S ADMIRERS

Sing little box

Don't let sleep get the better of you
The whole world is awake within you

In your four-square emptiness
We turn distance into closeness
Oblivion into memory

Don't let your nails go loose

Through your keyhole
We see for the very first time
Regions beyond the world

We turn your key in our mouths
And gulp down letters and numbers
From your song

Don't let your lid fly off
Don't let your bottom drop out

Sing little box

THE LITTLE BOX'S WORKMEN

Don't open the little box
The sky's cap will fall out

Don't shut her whatever you do
She'll cut eternity's trouser-leg off

Don't drop her on the ground
The sun's eggs will get smashed inside

Don't throw her into the air
The earth's bones will get broken inside

Don't hold her in your hands
The star-dough will go sour inside

For God's sake mind what you're doing
Don't let her out of your sight

THE LITTLE BOX'S OWNERS

Line the little box
With your own precious skin
And make yourself
At home in her

Ride space in her
And pick stars and milk time
And sleep on clouds

Just don't go acting
More important than her length
And cleverer than her width

Or we'll flog you off you and her
And everything inside her for a song
To the first swindler of a wind

We don't give a toss for profit
We don't stock damaged goods

And stop telling everyone
We're talking to you
From inside the little box

THE LITTLE BOX'S HIRERS

Throw a stone
Into the little box
And you'll pull out a bird

Throw in your shadow
And you'll pull out the shirt of happiness

Throw in your father's root
And you'll pull out the axis of the world

The little box will work for you

Throw a mouse
Into the little box
And you'll pull out a golden mountain-shaker

Throw in your mother's shell
And you'll pull out the chalice of immortality

Throw in your head
And you'll pull out two

The little box will work for you

THE LITTLE BOX'S ENEMIES

Don't bow down before the little box
Who allegedly has everything inside her
Your star and all the rest as well

Empty yourselves
In her emptiness

Pull all her nails out
And give them to her owners
So they can eat them up

Knock a hole through her middle
And stick her on your clapper

Stuff her with plans
And her builders' skin
And trample her underfoot

Tie her to a cat's tail
And chase the cat away

Don't bow down before the little box
Or you won't be able
To get up again

THE LITTLE BOX'S VICTIMS

Mind you have nothing to do
With the little box
Even in your sleep

If you've seen her full of stars
You'll wake up
With an empty chest no heart no soul

If you've stuck your tongue
Up her keyhole
You'll wake up with your forehead full of holes

If you've crunched her
Between your teeth
You'll wake up with a square head

If you've seen her empty
You'll wake up
With a belly full of nails and mice

If you've had anything to do with the little box
In your dreams
You're better not waking up at all

THE LITTLE BOX'S JUDGES

for Karl Max Ostojić

Why are you gawping at the little box
Who's got the whole goddam world
In her emptiness

If the little box holds
The world in her emptiness
Then the unworld holds
The little box in its unhand

Who'll bite off the unworld's unhand
And its unhand's
Five hundred unfingers

Do you really think
You can bite them off
You with your thirty-two teeth

Or are you waiting
For the little box to jump
Into your mouth all by herself

Is that why you're gawping

THE LITTLE BOX'S BENEFACTORS

We'll give the little box
Back to the embrace
Of her decent little features

We won't upset her
In the slightest
We'll just take her to bits

We'll crucify her
On her own cross

We'll pop her puffed-up emptiness
Let all the blue cosmic blood she's hoarded up
Trickle out of her

We'll cleanse her
Of stars of anti-stars
Of all that stuff rotting away inside her

We won't torment her
We'll just put her back together

We'll give the little box
Her own pure littleness back again

THE LITTLE BOX'S PRISONERS

Open up little box

We're kissing your bottom and lid
Your keyhole and key

The whole world has barged inside you
And now it looks like anything
But itself

Serenity its own mother
Wouldn't recognize it now

Rust will eat up your key
Our world and us inside you
And you too in the end

We're kissing all four of your sides
And all four of your corners
And all twenty-four of your nails
And everything you've got

Open up little box

LAST NEWS OF THE LITTLE BOX

The little box with the whole world inside
Fell in love with herself
And conceived inside herself
Another little box

The little box's little box
Fell in love with herself too
And conceived inside herself
Another little box

And so on ad infinitum

The little box's whole world
Should be somewhere
Inside the little box's last box

None of the little boxes
In the little box in love with herself
Is the last one

Try finding the world now

TRANSLATOR'S AFTERWORD

The first appeal of Vasko Popa's poetry in translation is its strange-
ness; he seems to observe with a scientific detachment the processes
of a universe parallel yet alien to ours – one where pebbles fall in love,
where limetrees grow in people's hearts, where blue and black suns
are born from heaven's armpit, where the constellation of the Wolf
rides high in the sky.

But there is more to Popa than the disturbing surface of
his imagery. His words and images are multilayered, combining
concrete representation with idiomatic, proverbial and atavistic
meanings to form complex, archetypal signs, which interpret more
levels of existence than what is merely tangible in this or another
universe.

Many of Popa's images, though his own inventions, have the
timeless quality of elemental archetypes, interpreting existence at the
level of the species – the sunflower, for example:

> He was simply out of this world they say
> He had gone to find the sunflower
> In which meet the paths
> Of every heart and every star
>
> (from 'The Starmaster's Death')

Not all of Popa's archetypes are invented, however: he also takes half-
forgotten images from his people's past and involves them in his own
poetic cosmogony. An example is St Sava from *Earth Erect* and *Wolf
Salt*, who bears little resemblance to the historical personage, but
rather more to the figure from the folk-tales, who has in his turn
taken on the attributes of various pre-Christian Slav deities and
animistic cults. The wolf, for example, was the totem of some South

Slav tribes, and the god Dabog was the wolves' protector — a role
which St Sava took over in folk belief:

> To his left flows time
> To his right flows time
>
> He strides over dry land
> Escorted by his wolves

(from 'St Sava')

These atavistic leitmotifs (which have greater prominence in Popa's
middle and later work) occur even in the superficially 'realistic'
poems of *The Cut*, for instance, showing that modern man, alienated
though he feels, is linked to his ancestral past by a chain of symbol:

> I'm having breakfast in my flat with a cousin
> Wolf from green Sand
>
> He licks the honey from his bare clasp-knife
> And reveals to me
> The shining alphabet of his teeth

(from 'Breakfast in the Big City')

Indeed, Popa is less of a scientist than an alchemist. Mixing signs from
our language and elements from our universe in the alembic of his
verse, he seeks correspondences instead of compounds, images
instead of observations, truths instead of facts. The mediaeval alche-
mist's real quest, after all, was not for gold the metal (this was a fable
to fob off the idly curious) but for gold the symbol, the core and
essence of existence. In a universe of symbols, of images, physical
relationships are rearrangeable according to the rules of analogy, of
correspondances – rules which may express truths of a different order
to those on the surface of things:

> They yell about water being H_2O
> And don't dream that clouds
> Are planets too

(from 'Dispute about Dew')

Popa's skill as a poet does not only lie in his imagery. Although he eschews rhyme and rigidity of rhythm, his verse is highly crafted in sound terms; in the original, his lines are limpid, jewel-like – anything but crudely mimimalist, in fact. One does not need to know Serbo-Croat to hear a master poet at work:

Providan *go*lub u *gla*vi
U *go*lubu *gli*nen *kov*čeg
U *kov*čegu *mrt*vo *mo*re
U *mo*ru *bla*žen *me*sec
('A Dove in the Head', lines 1–4: stressed syllables in italics)

I have tried to reproduce Popa's phonic texture where possible in my own translations, although I have given higher priority to an exact rendering of his images and of his easy, colloquial style.

At times, however, Popa's imagery itself is so rich and multilayered that we, his translators, cannot manage to capture all its levels. Footnotes are held by many to be second-rate solutions to translation problems, but the sheer complexity of Popa's poetry has often left us with no alternative; and even if the complexity has been captured, the full effect of Popa's imagery may only be apparent in the light of typically Serbian or Slavic assumptions and associations about the world. Hence the following pages, which aim to supply a commentary on points where the English reader would otherwise miss out.

Since I first wrote these notes, Tito's Yugoslavia, which Vasko Popa so passionately believed in, has been bloodily dismembered by brutish, blood-and-soil nationalisms. Serbian nationalism exploits the same cultural heritage that Popa so sensitively explores – but its aim is to justify a hatred of the other, not to gain a deeper understanding of the self. Let the two not be confused.

FRANCIS R. JONES
1994

NOTES ON THE POEMS

xxxiii Anne Pennington
  'limetrees': the limetree (linden) is a Serbian national symbol.

BARK

4 *Conversation*
  'buried river': *ponornica* denotes a river that disappears into the earth and reappears again.

11 *In the Ashtray*
  'Beheaded': *obezglavljena* also means 'giddy, confused'.

21 *LIST*
  The format of this cycle is that of the folk-riddle – except that the answers are given in the titles.

38 *Far Within Us 2*
  'unrest-field': *nepočin-polje*, which Popa used as the title of a later collection of poems, is only mentioned in one dictionary, that of Vuk Karadžić (1819), and he only reports one occurrence of the term – in the riddle 'The dead bear the living across the unrest-field'. Karadžić unfortunately fails to give the answer to the riddle: a boat.

42 *Far Within Us 6*
  'beginning to singe / The fingers': *dogorela (je) do nokata* (literally: 'it's burnt down to the fingernails') is used idiomatically to mean 'things are getting desperate'.
  'dome of the sky': *nebeski svod*, which I have translated literally, is a standard collocation meaning 'the firmament'.

53 *Far Within Us 17*
'flowerbeds': *leje* also means 'seed-drills'.

UNREST-FIELD

See note on *Far Within Us 2* above.

71 *Before Play*
Zoran Mišić: during the struggle for creative freedoms in the early 1950s, the critic, literary historian and anthologist Zoran Mišić (1921–1976) provided vital theoretical support for the young avant-garde, and was one of the first to recognize not only the originality, but also the excellence of Vasko Popa's verse. Ivan V. Lalić, another leading poet of the fifties generation, writes a moving, elegiac tribute to Zoran Mišić in *Rovinj Quartet* (in THE PASSIONATE MEASURE, Anvil, 1989).

96 *Give Me Back My Rags 3*
'distilled or double-distilled': *prepečen* literally means 'double-roasted', but is generally used in the context of brandy-making. *Prepečenica* is the best, 'double-distilled' brandy; many peasants, however, also make the much less fiery *meka rakija* ('mild brandy'), which is only distilled once.

98 *Give Me Back My Rags 5*
'harebrained puppets': *lutke* means both 'dolls, puppets' and 'whims'.

99 *Give Me Back My Rags 6*
'fire-eyes': *žar-okca* reminds one of *Žar-ptica* – the Firebird.
'symbol': *znamen* also means 'banner'.

101 *Give Me Back My Rags 8*
'hair': *pramen* means both 'a lock, tuft' (of hair) and 'a wisp' (of fog).

105 *Give Me Back My Rags 12*
'hawthorn stake': according to Serbian folk-beliefs, a hawthorn stake had to be driven through a vampire's heart to prevent it from rising from the dead.

107 *THE QUARTZ PEBBLE*

I once read in a compendium of folklore that, in certain parts of Serbia, *beluci* (quartz pebbles) were believed to contain the souls of the dead, and hence were worn as amulets. Eager to show off my research, I mentioned this to Vasko Popa. He replied that this was the first he had heard of such a belief – but then he thanked me warmly, for it showed how his choice of image had in reality been anything but random!

110 *The Love of the Quartz Pebble*

'cost him his head': *doći (mu) glave* (literally 'come for his head') is a highly colloquial expression, akin to the English 'do him in'.

SECONDARY HEAVEN

117 *The Star-Gazer's Legacy*

'star-gazer': *zvezdoznanac* ('star-knower') is an old-fashioned term for *astronom* ('astronomer').

125 *An Intruder*

'sun': in Serbian folk-tales the Sun is often portrayed as a living being (probably indicating his worship as a deity in early times).

'fiery bread' / 'beakers of light': note the Christian symbolism. In Balkan popular mediaeval beliefs, such as the Bogomil heresy, Christ and the Sun were often closely identified – although Popa is possibly taking the Christ-figure right back to his origins as a Near Eastern solar deity.

'dead stars': the stars were often held to be the souls of the dead; cf. note to *The Warriors of the Blackbird's Field* below.

128 *A Homeless Head*

'To him it smiles': Serbo-Croat, like most Indo-European languages except for English, has 'grammatical' rather than 'natural' gender – hence *mesec* ('moon') is a masculine noun (like *kompjuter* and *realizam*) and is referred to by the masculine pronoun. Whilst this does not necessarily imply personification, it does not rule it out either; English translators, by contrast, have to make an overt choice between personification ('he/she') and reification ('it'). If there *is* personification, however, it would go against the grain for a Serbo-Croat speaker to give the Moon feminine gender, as we would in English! In Serbian folk-belief, moreover, the Moon is the brother – or the uncle – of the Sun.

130 *Burning Hands*
'In the depths of heaven': *na pučini neba* (literally 'on the high seas of the sky/heaven') is a common idiom meaning 'in the skies'.

133 *A Crowned Apple*
'sun' / 'apple': in Slav folk-tales the apple (often golden) usually symbolizes the Sun, who is sometimes portrayed holding an apple in his hand – cf. THE GOLDEN APPLE (Anvil, 1980), Vasko Popa's collection of folk-tales.

141 *IMITATION OF THE SUN*
The title of the cycle underlines the Sun-Christ parallel mentioned above (v. note to *An Intruder*).

141 *Death of the Sun's Father*
'limetree': see note to *Anne Pennington* above.

143 *Clash at the Zenith*
'tripod': a *tronožac* is any three-legged object; hence it could also denote a three-legged stool (as in *The Suffering of the Golden Stool*).

147 *Imitation of the Sun*
'apple-bearer': cf. note to *A Crowned Apple* above.

150 *A Cake of Ashes*
'crossed daggers': knives, especially crossed, protect one against evil spirits – cf. *The Betrothed of Death* (in THE CUT).

151 *An Extinguished Wheel*
'wheel': a Slav sun-symbol.

157 *THE LIMETREE IN THE HEART*
Cf. note to *Anne Pennington* above.

161 *The Suffering of the Golden Stool*
See note to *Clash at the Zenith* above.

165 *The Star-Gazer's Death*
'trollops': *pokvarenice* could also mean 'perverts'.
'Did him in': *došle mu glave* – cf. note to *The Love of the Quartz Pebble* above.

166 *Heaven's Ring*
'ring': *prsten* means specifically 'a finger-ring' (American-English 'band').

EARTH ERECT

175 *PILGRIMAGE*
In this cycle the poet visits a number of shrines important in Serbian history.

175 *Pilgrimage*
'burning heart': note the Christian symbolism here.
'The constellation of the Wolf': the wolf was an ancient Slav totem – see Translator's Afterword. Cf. also note ('dead stars') to *An Intruder* above.

176 *Chelandarion*
Chelandarion (*Hilandar* in Serbo-Croat) is a Serbian monastery on Mount Athos, the 'Holy Mountain' in Northern Greece. In the late twelfth century Serbia was becoming a powerful nation-state. In 1192 Rastko, son of the Župan (ruler) Stefan I Nemanja, secretly ran away to Mount Athos, where he became a monk by the name of Sava; eventually his father abdicated and joined him there. With the support of the new ruler of Serbia, Sava's brother Stefan II, they founded the monastery of Chelandarion in 1198. Later Sava returned to Serbia, becoming the first Archbishop of the newly autonomous Serbian Orthodox Church – and eventually, after his death, his country's

patron saint. For centuries Chelandarion remained the spiritual centre of the Serbian people.

'black Three-Handed Mother': Chelandarion contains a miraculous icon, blackened with age, of the Three-Handed Virgin – so called because she has a silver votive hand in addition to her two painted ones.

'magic ocean': Mount Athos is one of the three narrow peninsulas at the tip of Chalcidice; Chelandarion is a half-hour's walk from the sea.

'a thousand mists': one of several etymologies for the monastery's name claims that it derives from the Greek *chiliai antarai*, or the 'thousand mists' which sometimes roll down from the surrounding hills.

177 *Kalenić*

After their defeat of the Balkan Christian armies at the Field of the Blackbirds (*Kosovo polje*) in 1389 (see THE BLACKBIRD'S FIELD cycle and notes), the Ottoman Turks were unable to follow up their victory because of the incursions of Tamburlaine in the East. In the ensuing lull, Serbia, though officially an Ottoman vassal state, still had a certain illusory degree of control over its own destiny. Under the rule of the Despot Stefan Lazarević, several fine monasteries were built, among them Kalenić (between about 1407 and 1413). Any Serbian dreams of independence, however, were shattered with the rallying of the Ottoman Empire under Mohammed II the Conqueror, culminating in the fall of Constantinople in 1453 – upon which, in 1459, Serbia became an Ottoman province.

'your sword': Kalenić, like most Serbian monasteries, contains many beautiful frescoes, including those of warrior saints.

178 *Žiča*

This monastery was founded by Stefan II Nemanja in 1208 as his coronation church; when the Serbian Orthodox Church gained autonomous status in 1219, Archbishop Sava finally crowned Stefan, his brother, there as the first King of Serbia – who from then on bore the title Prvovenčani, or 'First-Crowned'.

'crimson lady': the church is painted red, the colour of royalty.
'seven-gated': seven kings were crowned in Žiča, and for each a
new door was specially built. Cf. also note ('seven more steps')
to *Szentendre* below.
'the sun your bridegroom': cf. notes to *An Intruder* above. Once
again, Popa identifies the Sun with Christ, implying that the Serbs'
pre-Christian and Christian pasts are really a single heritage.
'fiery triangle': Žiča, as the archiepiscopal seat of the Serbian
Orthodox church, was held by Serbs to be equal to St Peter's in
Rome and Agia Sofia in Constantinople, the three shrines
forming a triangle with Žiča at its peak.
'the sun-slayer / And the corn-defiler': Žiča suffered dreadfully
at the hands of the Austrians in the First World War and the
Nazis in the Second, although it has now been extensively
restored.

179 *Sopoćani*
This monastery, founded in 1260, also dates from Nemanja
times; it is famous for the beauty of its frescoes, which have
survived in spite of the church having remained roofless for
centuries.

180 *Manasija*
This fortified monastery was built by Stefan Lazarević, Despot
of the Serbian vassal state (see note to *Kalenić* above) between
about 1406 and 1418 as his mausoleum; he also held court here.
When the Turks finally put an end to Serbian autonomy in
1459, Manasija was overrun and the Turks stabled their horses
in the church, destroying all frescoes up to shoulder height.
Despite centuries of neglect and misuse of the church (the
Austrian 'liberators' in the early eighteenth century – cf. note
to *Szentendre* below – used it as a powder magazine), most of
the wonderful frescoes have survived.

181 *Szentendre*
After the Turks tried unsuccessfully to take Vienna in 1683, the
Austrians went on the counter-offensive, liberating Hungary.
This sparked off uprisings in the Balkans, and the Austrians

even briefly liberated Belgrade and – a few years later (1718–1739) – Northern Serbia. In 1690 the defeat by the Turks of an Austrian army in which Serbian volunteers were fighting caused a massive migration of Serbs northwards into Hungary. Szentendre ('St Andrew's') on the Danube north of Budapest became an important centre of Serbian trade, religion and culture.

'seven more steps': the number seven plays an important role in Popa's symbolic universe. Many cycles (such as this one) are made up of seven poems; the book SECONDARY HEAVEN is made up of seven cycles of seven poems each.

'the river of paradise': 'And a river went out from Eden to water the garden; and from thence it was parted, and became into four heads. The name of the first is Pison: that is it which encompasseth the whole land of Havilah, where there is gold.' (Genesis ii, 10–11). Slav exegesists took Pison to be the River Danube.

'old-men oaks': the oak was a sacred tree of the ancient Slavs, its cult surviving (with a Christian veneer) into comparatively recent times; it was sacred to Perun, the god of thunder. Once again we see a fusion of Christian and pagan symbolism, demonstrating the unbroken thread of Serbian culture.

'iris flower': the iris (*perunika*) was, as its name suggests, also sacred to Perun.

183 *ST SAVA'S SPRING*
The Sava of this cycle is not the historical prince-archbishop (see notes to *Chelandarion* and *Žiča*), but the folk-figure and patron saint of Serbia. St Sava's rather curious collection of attributes, tasks and miracles in folk-belief result from his having taken over many features of pre-Christian deities.

183 *St Sava's Spring*
Savin izvor (Sava's Spring) is a common spring-name in Serbia; these springs were considered to be healing.

'the staff's fourfold kiss': at the touch of St Sava's magic staff, water would flow from the stone.

'the crystal wolf-head': in Serbian legend, St Sava is the 'wolf shepherd', the protector of the wolves, a Slav totem animal (cf. Translator's Afterword and notes to *St Sava's Pastoral Work*). This is a role he has taken over from the Slavic god Dabog; as the souls of dead people were thought to inhabit wolves, Dabog was also god of the dead.

'With a rainbow in its jaws': the thunder-god Perun (cf. notes to *Szentendre* above), who brought the storm, rain and the rainbow, also – like St Sava – gave his name to many springs.

184 *The Life of St Sava*
'He tended their golden-fleeced clouds': like Perun, St Sava was believed to lead the storm-clouds. If hail threatened, one had to shout into the sky: 'St Sava, send your flock back from our village!', and thunderstorms on St Sava's day were believed to herald great upheavals in the land.

'He lives without years without death': St Sava was held to be immortal.

185 *St Sava*
'bees' / 'He strides over dry land': St Sava was a travelling saint; like the god Dabog, he journeyed through the world, teaching people many skills, including that of beekeeping.

'chains': besides a staff, St Sava was usually held to carry a chain.

'his cock': sacred to St Sava.

186 *St Sava's Pastoral Work*
One legend tells how St Sava changed a shepherd and his flock to stone, his hounds to wolves, and the cream from the sheep's milk to scree. Paradoxically, perhaps, St Sava was also said to have taught people how to make cheese and yoghurt. Another legend says that on his saint-day he sits in the top of a pear tree and summons his flock of wolves; he then feeds them and tells them which sheepfolds to raid in the following year.

'To give birth': besides making water flow from the stone, St Sava's magic staff could perform a host of other tasks, including opening locked doors, helping women give birth, and creating bears, wolves and squirrels!

187 *St Sava's Forge*
St Sava, like the god Dabog, taught men how to forge metal.

188 *St Sava's School*
'pear tree' / 'wolves': see note to *St Sava's Pastoral Work* above.
'The book of the lord of the world' / 'white lambs': note the
Christian symbolism here.

189 *St Sava's Journey*
'He flings... / At the grey army of mice': one legend tells how St
Sava was travelling in a dark land ravaged by a plague of mice;
St Sava then changed his glove into a cat, which got rid of them
all. It is believed that the 'dark land' represents the underworld
and the mice the shades of the dead: another link with Dabog,
the god of the dead (cf. notes to *St Sava's Spring*).
'storm': see note to *The Life of St Sava*.
'chains': see note to *St Sava*.
'the ancient oaken land': see note to *Szentendre* above.
'the fixed stars': see note to *An Intruder* above.

190 *St Sava at His Spring*
'St Sava at His Spring' (*Sveti Sava na svom izvoru*) could also
mean 'St Sava at His Source/Origin'.
'His pillaged coffin': after the historical St Sava's death, his
bones were removed to the monastery of Mileševo, which
became a place of pilgrimage and a focus of Serbian conscious-
ness. They were removed by the Turks in 1594 and burnt
publicly on Vračar Polje ('The Apothecaries' Field') in Bel-
grade.

191 *THE BLACKBIRD'S FIELD*
Popa's poems and cycles are frequently arranged symmetri-
cally about a central 'pivot': the central position of *THE BLACK-
BIRD'S FIELD* in the book (number 3 of 5) implies that it is the
key cycle. The key poem of this cycle of seven poems (cf. note
to *Szentendre* above) is therefore *The Battle on the Blackbird's
Field*. See also note to *THE TOWER OF SKULLS* below.

Under Stefan Dušan (ruled 1331–1355), Serbia had become the leading power in the Balkans, but his Empire disintegrated into petty, feuding principalities ('despotates') after his death. Knez ('Prince') Lazar of Raška (Serbia proper) managed to weld together an anti-Turkish alliance, but the Christian armies were decisively defeated at Kosovo Polje – the Field of the Blackbirds – in 1389, both commanders (Lazar and Sultan Murat II) dying in the battle. Although direct Turkish occupation did not follow for 70 years (see note to *Kalenić* above), the power of Serbia was broken for good. The battle and the legends surrounding it, which are celebrated in a magnificent cycle of folk epics, are still of enormous emotive value to the Serbs.

191 *The Blackbird's Field*
'Peonies': legend has it that the white peonies which grew upon the Plain of Kosovo were stained red with the warriors' blood.

192 *Supper on the Blackbird's Field*
The banquet on the eve of the battle occurs in several folk epics; note also the parallels with Christ's Last Supper.
'the stars in each others' hearts': the stars were held to be the souls of the dead; cf. note to *The Warriors of the Blackbird's Field* below.
'Their ruby future': one legend tells how, just before the battle, Prince Lazar was asked to choose between an earthly and a heavenly empire – and he chose the latter, sealing his and his warriors' earthly fate.

194 *The Battle on the Blackbird's Field*
'wolf shepherd': St Sava – see notes above.
'Flies through the air on his white steed': Popa has merged St Sava with Svetovid, known as 'the White', the Slav god of light and of battle, who rides through the sky on a horse.
'our betrothed stars': see note to *The Warriors of the Blackbird's Field* below.

195 *The Crowned One of the Blackbird's Field*
Prince Lazar was eventually canonized by the Serbian church –
because he was already the focus of a folk-cult.
'benefaction': *zadužbina* could also be translated as 'endow-
ment'; the endowers of a church were usually depicted on a
fresco, holding a model of the church in their hand.

196 *The Warriors of the Blackbird's Field*
'his namesake star': in Serbian folklore, each person has his or
her own star, which is born with the person, travels as they
travel, and disappears as they die. A variant, already men-
tioned, has it that the stars are actually the souls of the dead.

197 *The Blackbird's Mission*
'Bears off in his beak': in several folk epics, news of the battle is
borne to the womenfolk by ravens – in *The Death of the Jugovići's
Mother (Smrt majke Jugovića)*, for example, the mother is only
able to grieve when two ravens bring her her youngest son's
hand. Popa has fused the ravens of the epics with the blackbird
of the field's name.

199 THE TOWER OF SKULLS
It was only in the nineteenth century that the Serbs began to
wrest their freedom from the Turkish occupiers. The First
Serbian Uprising (1804–1812) was led by the charismatic
Karađorđe ('Black George'). In 1809 his forces suffered a defeat
at the Battle of Čegar: the Serbian commander Sindželić, hope-
lessly outnumbered, exploded an ammunition store, destroy-
ing his own men with the enemy. After the battle, the Turks
built a tower encrusted with the skulls of the Serbian dead. Still
standing, it is known as *Ćele-kula*, the Tower of Skulls.
    This cycle is a good example of symmetrical structure
(see note to THE BLACKBIRD'S FIELD above): the first and last
poems (*The Tower of Skulls* and *The Song of the Tower of Skulls*)
are thematically linked, as are the second and penultimate, etc.

199 *The Tower of Skulls*
'the châtelaine': death. *Smrt* is a feminine noun and thus (see

discussion on 'moon' in note to *A Homeless Head* above) considered to be a female figure. Cf. also *The Betrothed of Death* from THE CUT.

200 *Initiation of Black George*
'his holy king': Knez Lazar (cf. notes to THE BLACKBIRD'S FIELD above).
'The oaken planks': see note to *Szentendre* above.
'guiding stars': i.e. the souls of his ancestors.

201 *Black George*
'my head is watching me': cf. note to *The Death of Black George* below.
'my wolves': cf. Translator's Afterword.

204 *The Death of Black George*
The Second Serbian Uprising, under the leadership of the pragmatic, ruthless and cunning Milos Obrenović, began in 1815. When Karađorđe returned to Serbia in 1817, Obrenović, fearing that Karađorđe would take over the leadership of the Uprising, had Karađorđe murdered and sent his head to Constantinople in order to ingratiate himself with the Sultan. Eventually Serbia won full autonomy from the Turkish Empire in 1830 – but it is debatable whether the population was actually any better off under Obrenović's autocratic, corrupt and unpopular rule. The feud between the two royal dynasties, the Karađorđevići and the Obrenovići, is an obsessive thread running through the next century of Serbia's history.
'flutes': *frule*, the peasant pipes, not the orchestral *flaute*.

207 *Return to Belgrade*
'this cross of water': Belgrade is built at the confluence of the Sava and the Danube.
'the river of paradise': the Danube – see note to *Szentendre* above.
'the Sun Mother': in Serbian folk-tales, the Sun figure (see note to *An Intruder* above) only had a mother, and not a father. Her name, *suncorodica*, reminds one of *bogorodica*, the Christian Mother of God.

'white town': the literal meaning of *Beograd* (Belgrade). Here, however, it could also mean 'white hail'.

208 *The Upper Fortress*
The heart of Belgrade is the Kalemegdan Fortress on the promontory overlooking the confluence of the two rivers.
'you the Tall': the Serbian Despot Stefan Lazarević (see notes to *Kalenić* and *Manasija* above), who conquered Belgrade from the Hungarians in 1402 and rebuilt its fortresses, was nicknamed 'Stefan the Tall'.
'From your verses' / 'word of love': *Slovo ljubavi* ('The Word of Love') is the title of an important poetic work by Stefan Lazarević.

209 *Terazije*
Terazije ('The Scales') is the central square of Belgrade.

210 *Apothecaries' Field*
See note to *St Sava at His Spring* above.

211 *Fearless Tower*
The octagonal *Nebojša kula*, or 'Fearless Tower', stands below the Kalemegdan Fortress at the exact point where the Sava and the Danube join. Legend has it that this is the centre of the forces of Good, which fly out every night to do battle with the forces of Evil (which are based in Avala, a few kilometres outside the city) so that day may triumph.
'the thunderer': the god Perun; see also notes to *Szentendre* and *St Sava's Spring*.

213 *Belgrade*
Belgrade has been destroyed by many invaders, only to rise again – the last occasion was the Nazi Luftwaffe raid in April 1941.

WOLF SALT

This work explores a theme already touched on in earlier poems: the wolf, a totem of the ancient Slav tribes, symbolizes the South Slav people.

217 *THE WORSHIPPING OF THE LAME WOLF*
This cycle could be seen as depicting the conversion of the Slav tribes to Christianity. The speaker is St Sava ('the wolf shepherd') and the 'lame wolf' represents pre-Christian beliefs – which Christianity, personified in St Sava, does not reject, but respectfully absorbs. The dogs are perhaps the Byzantines, the bringers of Christianity, but they could also represent any of Serbia's historical occupiers.

219 *The Worshipping of the Lame Wolf 3*
'irises': see note to *Szentendre* above.

221 *The Worshipping of the Lame Wolf 5*
'deer with gold antlers': in the village of Jablanica in Serbia, legend has it that the villagers used to lay out sacrificial offerings on a hillside every year for a stag with golden antlers. One year the villagers forgot, so the stag ordered that he should be sacrificed instead. Since then – and to this day – a sheep has been sacrificed on the same hillside.

222 *The Worshipping of the Lame Wolf 6*
'Three wonder-working hairs': wolf-hairs were used as amulets or in folk-medicine.

225 *THE FIERY SHE-WOLF*
The she-wolf could be said to represent the Serbian land, wounded and ravaged by invaders, but throwing off her enemies in the end.

231 *PRAYER TO THE WOLF SHEPHERD*
The speakers, the wolves, are the oppressed people of Serbia under foreign overlordship. The structure of the poems is modelled on the Orthodox liturgy.

234 *Prayer to the Wolf Shepherd 4*
'our mother's / Crystal womb / Crammed with dog-seed': the amalgam of pagan and Christian culture – cf. note to *THE WORSHIPPING OF THE LAME WOLF*.

235 *Prayer to the Wolf Shepherd 5*
'the great grey cloud': see note to *The Life of St Sava* above.

237 THE WOLF LAND
This cycle's 'pivot position' in the book (see note to THE BLACK-BIRD'S FIELD above) implies that it is the key cycle. Concerned not with the foreign occupier but with the Slavs themselves, it revolves round the young Serb's question: will the age-old power of the wolf mean the salvation or the destruction of the Serbian land? Even the past, his father, has no answers. As the world now knows all too well, Serbian and Yugoslav history is not only a tale of glory, defeat and resistance. It is also characterized by periods of savage internecine struggle: though he died before the bloody break-up of Tito's Yugoslavia, Vasko Popa lived through the vicious three-way civil war that formed a background to the national liberation struggle against the Axis powers in the Second World War (cf. notes to THE BLACKBIRD'S FIELD and *The Death of Black George* above).

237 *The Wolf Land 1*
'the three-headed sun' (*troglavo sunce*): Triglav, 'The Three-Headed One', was the Slav god of light.

243 HYMN TO THE WOLF SHEPHERD
Cycles 3 and 5, flanking the central cycle, are related by their liturgical structure: cf. note to THE TOWER OF SKULLS above.

243 *Hymn to the Wolf Shepherd 1*
'A swarm of bees': see note to *St Sava* above.

249 THE LAME WOLF'S TRACKS
Despite the efforts of alien cultures, the ancient pagan heritage lives on.

251 *The Lame Wolf's Tracks 3*
'*gusle*': a South Slav folk-instrument, similar to a one-stringed viol, used to accompany the chanting of the folk epics. It is usually made of maplewood, and the peg-box ends in a carved horse's head.

252 *The Lame Wolf's Tracks 4*
'black eagle': possibly referring to the old (royalist) Serbian
coat of arms.

255 THE WOLF BASTARD
The wolf bastard is the modern Serb, who must deal with the
complexity of present-day life, speaking to his enemies, the
dogs – who represent not only the inhumanity of his country's
invaders, but also those robbed of their humanity by modern
mechanized civilization.

258 *The Wolf Bastard 4*
'anvil' / 'chain' / 'cloud': all linked to St Sava – see notes to *St.
Sava's Forge*, *St Sava* and *The Life of St Sava* above.

259 *The Wolf Bastard 5*
'Seven Sheepboys' (*Sedam Vlašića*): the Pleiades; according to
some, the seven Vlašići brothers are the souls of dead children.
Their name stems from that of the Slav god Volos – the god of
sheep, and of souls.
'crossed knifes': see note to *A Cake of Ashes* above.

RAW FLESH
This book and THE CUT are interesting in that the poems are not
arranged in cycles. There is still, however, a consciously symmetrical
layout in both books – they should 'open like wings', in Popa's words
– with the first and final poem, the second and penultimate poem,
etc. being linked thematically. Although these poems (and those of
THE CUT) are superficially workaday and anecdotal, the complex
symbolism of previous works is maintained, showing the unbroken
heritage linking the characters from Popa's home region with their
ancient cultural and mythic roots.

265 *Earthly Constellation*
Vršac, Popa's home town, is situated in the Banat area of Serbia
close to the Romanian border.
'star-gazer' (*zvezdoznanac*): cf. the poems *The Star-Gazer's
Legacy* and *The Star-Gazer's Death* from SECONDARY HEAVEN.

413

'To find my star its place too': see note to *The Warriors of the Blackbird's Field*.

266 *The Idol of Vršac*
This recently-discovered prehistoric idol is mentioned in *The Beautiful God-Hater* (THE CUT).
'Vrščanin': a native of Vršac (plural = Vrščani).

268 *The Unknown Citizen*
'astroragler' (*sic*): *astrogolja* is formed from *astrolog* and *golja*, someone too poor to clothe himself.

270 *The Lost Red Boot*
'oaken coffin': see note ('old-men oaks') to *Szentendre* above.

276 *Imminent Return*
Veliki Bečkerek concentration camp, where Vasko Popa was imprisoned is only 40 kilometres from Vršac.

279 *At the Sign of the Wolves*
'pear tree': see note to *St Sava's Pastoral Work*.

283 *Wolf Eyes*
This is the central poem in RAW FLESH, and hence the 'pivot poem' of the whole work.

301 *Beautiful Nothingness*
Sterija: the poet and dramatist Jovan Sterija Popović (1806–1856).

THE HOUSE IN THE HIGHROAD

Literally: 'The House in the Middle of the Highroad' (*Kuća nasred druma*); the house is, of course, Yugoslavia, astride the highroad from Europe to Asia Minor.

305 *HOUSEGUARD*
The title is a literal translation of *čuvarkuća*, which, besides meaning 'a caretaker', also refers to the stonecrop or houseleek, a wild flower which grows on stone walls and houses. In the South Slav lands (as in Wales) it is thought to protect the house from lightning.

308 *Stećak*
The *stećci* are tombstones found in Bosnia and Hercegovina. Some of them are finely carved with strange motifs, one being a man with an enormous upraised hand and a stylized sun instead of a head. Although they are usually assumed to have been carved by the adherents of the Bogomil heresy (cf. note to *An Intruder* above), their exact origins – and the meaning of many of the carvings – remain a mystery.

311 *Novi Sad: New Orchard in Blossom*
The city of Novi Sad ('New Orchard') lies on the Danube at the beginning of the great Pannonian Plain which covers most of Hungary; across the river are the hills of the Fruška Gora and the Austrian citadel of Petrovaradin (Peterwardein). It is the capital of what used to be the Autonomous Serbian Province of Vojvodina ('The Dukedom'), a multiethnic region with several languages, including Serbian, Hungarian, Romanian and Ruthenian.

321 *THE EYES OF SUTJESKA*
Sutjeska, a river in Hercegovina, was in May–June 1943 the scene of one of the fiercest battles fought by the partisans during the war.

THE CUT

See note to RAW FLESH.

341 *Breakfast in the Big City*
'Wolf': Vuk is a Serbian first name; see also Translator's Afterword.
'Sand': Pesak is the name of a village near Vršac – where a figure of an ancient god was discovered (see *The Idol of Vršac* in RAW FLESH, and cf. *The Beautiful God-Hater* from THE CUT).
'tree trunks': *balvani* has a number of different meanings, all of which are alluded to here: 'logs', 'blockheads', 'rafters', and 'household gods' (wooden figures placed at the entrance to the ancient Slavic longhouses).

342 *Crazy Way Out*

'There's a plank loose in my head': literally 'that I've got a plank missing in my head' (*da mi nedostaje / Jedna daska u glavi*); this is equivalent to 'I've got a screw loose'.

'They'll bury me / In a box with the planks loose': literally 'That they'll bury me / In a coffin of three planks' (*Da će me sahraniti / U sanduku od tri daske*); this refers to the expression 'They buried him in a coffin of four planks', which means 'He had a pauper's burial'... but the madman, of course, has one plank missing!

'with my planks unhinged': literally 'without my fourth plank' (*bez četvrte daske*).

343 *The House*

'false sun': *zubato sunce* means literally 'toothed sun' – a graphic idiom for bright sunshine that is still bitingly cold.

344 *The Poplar and the Passer-By*

'love': literally 'soul' (*dušo*), a common term of endearment. Popa also consciously refers, however, to the ancient – or not so ancient – belief that trees have souls (cf. note to *Szentendre* above).

350 *Legend of the Big City*

'pigeon-lofts': traditional dovecotes in the Balkans are tall and cylindrical, with pointed roofs.

358 *The Beautiful God-Hater*

'Hewn from an oak trunk': see note to *Szentendre* above.

'a god / Recently dug up in Sand': see *The Idol of Vršac* (RAW FLESH) and note to *Breakfast in the Big City*.

360 *Poem in View*

Novi Sad: see note to *Novi Sad: New Orchard in Blossom* above. Novi Sad was the scene of dreadful massacres in the Second World War, and also a centre of Communist resistance. In 1979 Vasko Popa became a founder member of the Vojvodina Academy of Arts and Sciences in Novi Sad.

368 *Rastko Petrović's Grave*

Rastko Petrović (1896–1949) was a leading Serbian poet of the inter-war period. His bones were moved back to 'the old country' in 1985.

'cakes': the boiled-wheat and honey *kolači* of Balkan festivals (such as New Year) have remained unchanged for thousands of years: the cakes which the Ancient Greeks used to lay before the tombs of their ancestors were made to the same recipe.

369 *Poets' Refuge*
'flings out his arms / White with plaster': the gesture is that of an angel's benediction on a monastery fresco (frescoes, of course, are painted on wet plaster).

371 *The Betrothed of Death*
'Nailed to his easy chair': a literal translation of *prikovan za naslonjaču*, which reminds one of the idiom *prikovan za krevet*, or 'bedridden'.
'her': death is a female figure – cf. *The Tower of Skulls* (EARTH ERECT) and note.
'I can't howl': another reference to the wolf-totem.
'kitchen knife' / 'arms crossed': for protection against evil spirits – cf. note to *A Cake of Ashes* above.

374 *Limetree Revenants*
The *Lipe povratnice* of the title are, on the one hand, 'limetree ghosts', and on the other hand 'limetree returners' – those Serbian emigrés (the limetree being the Serbian national tree) who have returned to their native land.

375 *Trouble within Trouble*
The title *Muka u muci*, which I have translated literally, is an idiom similar to our 'double trouble', or: 'it never rains but it pours'.

IRON GARDEN

385 *The Little Box's Hirers*
'a golden mountain-shaker': an allusion to the saying 'the mountains shook and a mouse was born' – equivalent to our 'much ado about nothing'.

391 *Last News of the Little Box*

'When I was young, before the Second World War,' Vasko Popa once told a translators' workshop in Rotterdam, 'they sold little tins of shoe polish – Schollpasta, I think it was called. On the lid there was a horn of plenty, full of little tins of Schollpasta, each with a horn of plenty on the lid, and so on ad infinitum. I found this a fascinating concept, but the idea lay dormant for years, until it became the seed of this poem.' The Serbo-Croat word *kutija* refers to a small container – whether it is made of metal ('a tin') or wood ('a box') is irrelevant.

A GUIDE TO SERBO-CROAT PRONUNCIATION

Serbo-Croat, though it may be written in Cyrillic or Latin script, is one of the few European languages with a perfect one-to-one sound-letter system, which is a blessing for the foreign learner and the native schoolchild alike.

Stress is never word-final, and in words of three or more syllables is usually on the antepenultimate syllable. The letters have similar values to their English equivalents, except for the following:

Letter   As in…(nearest equivalent)

c	*tsetse*
č	*ch*ew
ć	*t*une (rapid speech)
đ	*d*ew (rapid speech)
g	a*g*o*g* (never as in *g*entle)
j	*y*o*y*o
r	strongly trilled, as in Scots; a longer trill can act as a vowel (e.g. Vršac)
š	*sh*e
ž	trea*s*ure

INDEX OF TITLES

All poems have been translated by Anne Pennington, unless indicated with
* (translated by Francis Jones) or † (translated by Anne Pennington with
substantial reworking by Francis Jones).

422